TRIUMPH OVER LIFE CHALLENGES

TURNING PAIN into BLESSING

MELINDA RIBNER

Email: Mindyribner@gmail.com
Website: www.Melindaribner.com

Sign up for monthly newsletter.
www.Melindaribner.com

Subscribe to Melinda Ribner You Tube channel for guided meditation, interviews and talks.
www.youtube.com@Melinda Ribner

Profits from this book are donated to Israeli charities to feed, heal and protect the holy people living in Israel.

Discounted and free copies are available to non-profit organizations to distribute to people who have experienced all kinds of trials and challenges.
Please contact via email above.

ISBN: 979-8-9906964-9-5

CONTENTS

REVIEWERS

"The call of a still small voice of heavenly urgency, delivered with profound gentleness: Melinda Ribner opens direct connection with our ancestral transformational wisdom. Exquisitely, softly, grounding us first in core texts, (Biblical, Talmudic, philosophic and kabbalistic), she then brings us right into the present with an offering of riveting heart-opening personal accounts of life-changing 'holy tears.'

Ribner does not stop there: she ventures further, into the personal world of reader, gifting us with the user-friendly meditations of a seasoned guide, such that the depths that this book gives voice to, can truly land."

Rabbi Dr. Leibish Hundert,
Yeshivat Simchat Shlomo Jerusalem Israel.

"Say goodbye to feeling like a victim and open to living more purposefully and peacefully. In this precious book, Mindy Ribner offers sacred teachings, tools and inspiring stories to help us just do that."

Rabbi Sam Intrator,
Kavannah Life Singles, former Rabbi of the Carlebach Synagogue in Manhattan.

"I have always wondered how some people are able to surmount life's most painful experiences, while others are crushed by the trauma. This powerful book does more than explain why. It gives us the tools to reconnect to deeper levels of ourselves and access the blessing of our own pure soul connection. Though filled with the wisdom of the sages, it is written from the heart, so it is easy to understand. The stories and practices from this book can help all of us to shift our lives and become blessings for each other. "

Judith Lief,
Meditation student of Melinda

"This is the book to reach for when seeking grounded wisdom, clear direction and lived spiritual guidance in the face of life's most difficult passages, including illness, abuse, loss and war. Few writers bring Ribner's depth of understanding of Jewish mystical sources together with such practical clarity."

Alana Ruben,
Creativity coach, writer, teacher and theater artist.

"This book needed to be born for people today. Both inspiring and practical, this book empowers its readers to live more fulfilling lives, no matter what has happened to them."

Tirzah Singer,
Jerusalem Rosh Chodesh teacher and musical composer.

AUTHOR TO READER

This book was conceived unexpectedly out of a moment of "holy tears". It was the last day of Passover, and I was in synagogue when I received the call for this book. To fit the many additions to the holiday service into a standard time frame, the prayers were particularly rushed on that day in a way that dismayed me. When the chanting of the *Song of Songs*, a sublime expression of God's love for the Jewish people — was performed in a loud, hurried, perfunctory, and callous manner, something inside me broke.

Tears streamed down my face, and I even had to leave the sanctuary. My pain was immense, not from a place of logic, but from a deep wound in my heart. I cried for the feeling that God wishes to bestow so much love upon us, yet we often lack the vessels to receive it. As my tears deepened, I realized I was also crying for myself. I felt a profound spiritual isolation, a longing for a connection and community that felt just out of reach.

I walked out of the synagogue that morning and immediately told my friend Margery that my next book would be entitled "Holy Tears" and that it would be about the process of turning pain into blessing. I knew that these holy tears were a call for me to birth something new and healing into the world. Over the years, I have come to appreciate how my holy tears opened gates of blessing for me whenever I faced a hardship and challenge. My previous books were also mostly birthed out of experiences of holy tears.

The next day, I looked on Facebook and saw a post from Alana Ruben Free proclaiming that the people in Israel know how to turn pain into blessing. This was a sign for me. I contacted her. She was able to connect with me with people in Israel who went through challenge and who went on to be of service to others in ways that they would not have done otherwise. That was the primary criteria for inclusion of personal stories in this book.

Because not everyone would appreciate the power of holy tears without first reading this book, I decided to title the book "Turning Pain into Blessing". This title more clearly inspires potential readers to know that no one has to be limited or defined by challenge or trial. Furthermore, the challenges we face in life can even help access greater blessing in our lives.

P.S. Everyone is invited to sign up for my free newsletter and join in free meditation classes during the week at Melindaribner.com and view videos of free meditations and talks at Melinda Ribner You Tube channel.

INTRODUCTION

This book is written to offer a gateway through which pain, trauma, and challenge we experience can be transformed into blessing to oneself and others. The holy teachings, meditations, spiritual practices and inspirational stories in this book are designed to move the reader out of feelings of anxiety, despair, and victimhood into greater empowerment, love and gratitude for the precious time-limited gift of physical embodiment.

People often live our lives by a simple, powerful, and deeply flawed metric: whether an experience is good, bad, or neutral. When things feel good – a new job, a loving marriage, a recovered illness; we feel happy and fulfilled. We see life as a gift, a privilege to be enjoyed.

But life inevitably brings experiences we label as "bad." In the face of these trials, we are often overwhelmed by a flood of emotions: sadness, fear, anger, anxiety, and even shame. Embarrassed by the intensity of these feelings, many of us may try to hide them from ourselves and others, sometimes even turning to addictive behaviors to numb the pain.

When these emotions are active, we may engage in a torrent of unhelpful negative self-talk: "Something is wrong with me," "I'm not good enough," or "I will never be happy." 'What did I do to deserve such pain?" Why should I believe in God in light of what has happened?' Many of us begin to question everything, including our faith. We may judge ourselves as unworthy and feel cut off from a connection with God.

But what if our personal interpretation of "good" and "bad"

is incomplete? What if the very experiences that feel painful and negative are the ones that offer us the greatest opportunity to grow? What if these challenges are designed to help us live more authentically and purposefully, to become the people we are meant to be and fulfill our soul purpose? From this perspective, a "bad" experience might be a profound gift – one that deepens our compassion, strengthens our resilience, and inspires us to help others in ways we never thought possible.

This book does not aim to answer why people suffer or why bad things happen to good people. Rather it addresses these questions: In the face of challenges, how do we grow in trust and faith in the goodness of life and service to others, no matter what has happened in our lives? How do we access the wisdom of our own soul to guide us in a way no one or nothing else can? How do we deepen our capacity to love? How do we move forward in life?

As long as we are physically embodied, we each have an opportunity to raise our consciousness in positive and dramatic ways. It does not matter what religion we practice or do not practice, the teachings and stories in this book will offer spiritual nourishment to grow from the challenges we, as human beings, face personally and communally.

As we grow and heal, we may come to appreciate that our challenges and trials have been especially choreographed for our optimal spiritual growth in the time-limited period we are blessed to live in this physical world. Our suffering has not been a punishment but rather an initiation to a higher soul calling. The soul within us has been patiently waiting for us to give up trying to solve the problems of life on our own. One of the primary goals of this book is to help people access the inner peace and love that is integral to who they are on a soul level, regardless of what is happening to them or has happened to them previously.

Beyond offering fundamental teachings and meditations in

this book, it is the inspirational stories of readers like you, who rose from many different kinds of trials to be of greater service to others – that may likely be most important. Such stories help us to identify and better appreciate the spiritual and religious growth processes which empowered them to heal and go on to do something of greater service for others than they might have done otherwise without this trial or challenge.

There are a wide range of personal stories in this book. We do not need to have undergone a similar trial to learn and be inspired from these stories. Stories include that of Israelis who lived through the challenge of October 7th, hostages who grew in faith during their captivity, parents who lost children due to terrorism, war, illness and even suicide, stories of people who went through a variety of physical illnesses, women who left abusive marriages, rape, and much more.

As I read many of these stories, I myself cried holy tears. As it says in the Talmud, "Words of the heart enter the heart of another". I hope these stories will also break open your heart as well. It does not matter what our backgrounds are, when our hearts are open, we feel deeply for each other, the walls of separation crumble. We are united with each other. This sensitivity itself is a blessing and a key to receiving blessing in our lives.

My prayer is that this book will be a loving companion to all its readers to help heal and transform personal and communal pain, challenge, or trauma into living life with a deeper connection to the Creator. It is only there that we uncover the deeper strength, protection, compassion and inspiration to thrive in the midst of challenge and not to merely survive. The spiritual teachings and meditative practices when practiced, and not just read, will make a meaningful difference into living life with greater empowerment, every moment, in every day.

May we all come to appreciate that greater good and blessing came into the world because of how we grew through our trials, even if we will never be able to say that the trial itself was good or that we would have consciously chosen it. We each go through a variety of different life challenges because we have something important to share with others. Let this knowing empower us to embrace life purposely with gratitude.

I send my love and blessings for each reader to experience the blessing of God's love, especially when they are hurting.

I love you. It has been joy for me to write and share this book with others. So thank you for inspiring me. Thank you God for inspiring me.

Miriam Shulamit aka Melinda Mindy Ribner

CHAPTER 1

WHO, WHAT & WHERE IS GOD

Rabbi Bachya ibn Paquda in his masterwork *Duties of the Heart* offers a powerful analogy to persuade people to believe and trust in God. "How can one look upon the intricate tapestry of our world and believe it all came into existence by chance, without a Creator who formed and sustains it?"

He continues: "If ink were to be spilled accidentally onto a blank sheet of paper, would you expect to find coherent poetry? If you were handed such a paper, would you ever believe it was the result of an accident? Of course not... So too, when we look at the brilliance and intricacy of the universe, we must attest that it has a single creator who endowed it with purpose and imbued it with wisdom."

Nevertheless, I have heard people say that they do not believe in God because there is evil in the world. Consequently, they do not feel there is any meaningful purpose in prayer, crying, or talking to God. I have even met people who are challenged by the very mention of the word "God".

There are many more who say that they believe in the existence of a Divine Creator, but they do not believe that they can trust in God. Believing in God is quite different than trusting in God. The first is more of an intellectual idea; the second is a felt experience. This distinction changes our lives. To feel truly supported in challenging times, our belief must move from the head to the heart. It is only when we open to God – when we call out to God from the depths of our heart, when we surrender and align with Divine Will – God becomes real to us. The awareness of our divine connection expedites our personal transformation and empowers to do good in the world.

Before we move forward in exploring how to deepen our connection to the Creator and grow through challenge with trust and faith, it feels important to me to write about how to release limiting ideas of who and what God is – and who we are on a soul level. Too often, people rebel against the beliefs about God learned when they were children. These ideas may have been appropriate when we were young children, but they do not serve us as adults.

A great rebbe once said to people who did not believe in God, "The God you do not believe in, I also do not believe in." Our limiting and even false beliefs about God is the primary way we limit and even sabotage our capacity to receive blessings, especially when we are challenged. As you read this book, please open your heart and mind: Do not allow previous limiting concepts of God or even of yourself to interfere with the direct experience of God available to you now.

Judaism has always emphasized that there is only one God who is the Creator of all of creation. Interestingly enough, the Hebrew word for Israel (*Yisrael*) may be broken into two root words, *Yeshar* and *El*, which together means "straight to God". Every person, regardless of stature or religion, can have a relationship with God. According to Judaism, people of all faiths can be prophets and filled with the Holy Spirit. The Divine Presence is not discriminatory.

Because God is not physical and does not occupy space and time in the way that people do, many people do not know how to experience God within themselves, not even in the context of a relationship with this invisible Supreme Being. This is especially true in times of challenge. The *Zohar* calls God" The most hidden of all the hidden". It is true that God is hidden, but God is not distant. The Kotzker Rebbe tells us that" God is where you let God in." The prophet Isaiah reminds us, "All the world is full of God's glory.' The prophet Jeremiah speaks in the name of God. "Do I not fill heaven and earth." And, finally, my teacher Reb Shlomo Carlebach, of blessed memory, once said while reviewing one of my earliest books on Jewish meditation, "God is closer to you than your own breath."

The third commandment of The Ten Commandments actually forbids the making of images or pictures of God because God cannot be visualized or imagined. Yet, the Bible in the story of Genesis tells us, "Man is created in the image and likeness of God." This applies to every one of us. We have not been created to be frightened, powerless and limited beings. We are created in the image and likeness of God. Take a breath to absorb the power of this statement.

We have each been given a pure and holy soul; that is, in actuality, a part of God. This holy soul is who we really are, beyond our personal experience of ego or physical identity. When we access our soul, we connect with God, we raise our frequency and are better able to receive and radiate blessings to the world.

In his desire to increase intimacy and knowledge of God, Moses, the most exalted Jewish prophet, asks God, "What is your name? Who are You?" The answer of God in English means "I will be what I will be" This is considered the highest name of the Divine. This name "I will be what I will be" tells us that God is totally free and does not depend on anything else. No deficiency can be attributed to God. God has infinite potential. Will is the highest expression of the Divine. This is only time in the Torah that this name is revealed.

This Divine Name also reminds us that we are not victims of circumstance or powerless when we are attached to the Creator. We are not limited by our past nor our habits. Just as God is not constricted to the laws of cause and effect, when we are attached to God, we are also not constricted.

We are told that human beings have been gifted with free will. Our capacity to choose makes life meaningful and purposeful to us and to God. On the other hand, we are also told that God is in charge of this world and everything is divine providence. Do we make things happen in life or does God?

As we deepen our experiential connection with God, this paradox is resolved. Even though we may struggle with matters of faith and trust in the midst of challenge, the intention of this book is to help the reader appreciate that suffering is an invitation to grow in depth and in service. Everything in life offers opportunity to become a vessel with a greater capacity to receive and share the blessings of healing and abundance.

There are many more common names for God in Judaism. The most familiar name of God YHVH (pronounced *Adonai*) is rooted in the Hebrew word *hovey,* which means "to be". When the Hebrew letter *yud* is placed in front of the root it makes the verb active. So YHVH means 'Active Being" God is existence itself. God was, is and will be. The Hebrew language reminds us that only God has truly reality. In Hebrew, God is the only being who can say. "I am". For example, a person would say in Hebrew "I hungry". God is ultimately the Only True Reality. God is what makes everything alive.

The Torah teaches us that a person who attaches himself to

YHVH is "a person who is alive today" because God is the source of all life. When we meditate on this Hebrew name, our consciousness is lifted upward and our mind becomes very still.

The Divine Name *Adonai,* while meditating on the YHVH (known as the Tetragrammaton), is considered the key to all blessings in Judaism. We see this name used in the prayer book, providing an opportunity to meditate on it frequently. It is awesome and powerful to meditate on this Divine Name with focus and devotion.

If we feel unsteady or depressed, it is often because we place our trust in forces other than God. The Torah warns us very strongly about idolatry – how we can easily give our power away to what is not real, to what is limited and untrue. All too often, we foolishly put our faith in what we think we should want, in what we have achieved, or in what we can see, touch or feel in order to feel safe rather than in God. Yet nothing can offer us the blessing and security that consciousness of God can.

Our tendency for idolatry is not limited to what is external to us. People can even idolize themselves. When we form an image of ourselves that we feel we must live up to- even if it is not congruent with who we really are – this is a subtle form of idolatry. People even idolize God. We want God on our own terms, and for many, that is, merely a more romanticized or improved version of themselves. God should be everything we want God to be or we do not believe. The Torah tells us "God does good and creates evil." God in Judaism is not something sweet or sentimental but rather the underlying reality that encompasses good and evil.

Unfortunately, too often people allow their images of God and of themselves to separate themselves from the direct experience of the Divine. We benefit when we remember that our images are simply images, not God. To help us connect with God, sometimes we think of God as a person. He sees, He hears, He gets angry and He becomes sad. God is the Father, the Mother, the Friend, and the Lover. The Torah frequently even speaks of God in this manner. This may be helpful but if we get stuck in these limited ideas, we will never experience God as God. We only experience our own projections. It is important to be aware that God is beyond every definition, gender or name. If we try to define God, we limit our experience. To truly experience God, we must outgrow these limiting concepts of God.

For many of us it takes challenge, trial, loss and disillusionment to inspire us to let go of our illusions and align with God in a new and deeper way. In Judaism, challenges are called 'afflictions of love'. Our challenges are an initiation – an opportunity to better access our soul's potential. Furthermore, our capacity to grow in faith, trust and capacity for divine service expands, particularly when tested in times of immense pain.

Our suffering becomes a divine gift when it humbles us and helps us to surrender our sense of ego identity as a "victim". When we let go of experiencing ourselves in an ego – limited way, we stop trying to figure out life with our minds. We can then sit in the question of "What does God want of me now? "

When we stay in this question, we will be guided. We will be strengthened, purified and empowered. When we meditate upon this question and listen to what awakens within us, life opens up for us in unexpected ways.

Meditation and even prayer is not about reaching God who is so far away in heaven, sitting on a throne rewarding or judging us. Rather, they are about getting out of our own way and aligning with the Divine Presence that is so very close to us – a gateway to the experience of who we are on the level of our soul, wherever we happen to be.

As you read this book, I hope you remember to return your awareness to the breath from time to time and to the awesome gift of being alive and present in this moment of life, with gratitude, even when it may be challenging to do so.

Please keep your mind and heart open when reading and studying this book, especially if you are not yet a God believer or do not like meditation or prayer. Do your best always to love and respect yourself. If you are not currently facing a challenge, know that this book will help fortify you for inevitable challenges that life brings.

THREE MEDITATIVE PRACTICES TO EXPAND OUR EXPERIENCE OF GOD AND OUR OWN SOUL

1. BEGIN A DAILY PRACTICE OF BEING WITH ONE'S BREATH FOR AT LEAST FIVE MINUTES

It is a wonderful daily practice to take time each day to be consciously aware of the miraculous gift of life experienced in the breath. **We enter meditation when we become aware that we do not breathe by our own personal will but rather we are breathed by Divine Will. God is breathing us.** Our breath is gratefully not dependent on us remembering to breathe. Our very breath is a testament to our divine connection.

Every breath is a divine message that we matter, we are loved, and we are supposed now to be in a physical body. Every breath is precious. Be thankful for the gift of being physically embodied. When it is time for us to leave this physical plane of existence, we will no longer breathe.

God created us in such a way that our lives are dependent on the breath. When we become consciously attentive to the breath, the secrets of life itself are revealed to us. The inhalation teaches us about opening to receive, the space between the breath teaches us how to internalize what we have received and the exhalation teaches us about letting go of the past, regrets, anxiety and guilt. The more we can let go, the more we can open to receive. These secrets help us to live our lives with trust and faith, no matter what is happening in life. Conscious awareness of the breath also helps us to better receive the love and support contained within each breath.

Most importantly, consciousness on the breath brings our awareness into the present moment. We let go of the regrets of the past and concerns of the future. Stress and anxiety dissipates in the present moment. As we become more present, we open to the experience of being in the Presence; that is, the Divine Presence, the infinite love and light of the Creator. The experience of the Divine Presence becomes accessible to us only in the present moment. Give yourself time each day or night to meditate on the breath and the deeper truth that God is breathing and sustaining your life right now. Life then feels like a gift.

The Bible tells us "God made man of dust from the ground and breathed into his nostrils the breath of life and man became a living being." The *Tanya,* a major Chassidic commentary, expounds on this idea by teaching us that our soul comes from the depths of the Divine. The Tanya explains God's breath further by comparing the difference between the breaths which flows when one is speaking to that of forceful breathing.

The Tanya says. "When speaking, there is embodied within the breath only the smallest amount of the speaker's power and life force. But when he blows forcefully, he blows from deep within Himself. The breath embodies the internal power and life force of the vivifying soul."

To say that God breathed into man a pure soul shows that there is no separation or obstruction between God and man. "for if there were an obstruction, the exhaled breath of the Supreme One would not reach the human body." Breath means that there is a direct connection between God and the soul. The soul of a human being is not separate from God, but a part of God. Study this teaching deeply for this is a foundation for accelerated spiritual growth, protection and blessing.

If you like, during this breathing meditation, you can repeat the following words from the prayer book; "My God, the soul you placed within me is pure. You created it, You fashioned it, You breathed it into me."

When practicing this breathing exercise, make an effort to do slow conscious diaphragmatic breathing during some of the time of this breathing meditation. When the breath is brought down to the belly, the breath becomes longer and deeper, and we automatically feel more relaxed, centered and better able to tolerate all kinds of pain. The fewer breaths in a minute, the deeper we can go in meditation. Medical studies have documented that conscious slow deep breathing lowers blood pressure, strengthens the immune system, releases endorphins, natural chemicals in the brain, to produce a feeling of well-being and relaxation.

For those who are not accustomed to this type of breathing, it may be helpful to place your hands below the abdomen at first so you breathe into this part of the part. This is where we hold our deepest emotions, so please hold this part of your body with love and compassion. Make an effort to honor and be aware of any emotions or sensations that may arise without judgment, as fully and compassionately as possible. Do not fight or scold yourself for thoughts arising when you are in meditation. Those tendencies only strengthen the hold that the mind has in your consciousness.

If you find that the mind is thinking or judging, gently return the awareness to the breath. When we focus our awareness on the breath, the mind will begin to quiet and we can release the hold that self-criticism may have in our life.

If you become aware of tensions and sensations in the body during this meditation, gently breathe into the sensations. People often feel tension in part of the body that relate to the suppression of certain emotions. For example, people feeling tension in the chest usually need to release grief. People feeling tension in the back often need to release anger. When emotions and sensations are acknowledged and experienced, they lessen and dissipate.

When it is helpful, especially when the mind may become distracted, remind yourself that "Every moment is a new moment. God is with me in every breath. God is loving, supporting and sustaining me with every breath."

2. BE IN THE CENTER OF GOD MEDITATION

This following meditation has been adapted and simplified from the ancient mystical meditation text *Sefer Yetzirah*. This powerful meditation helps to free us of limiting anthropomorphic images of God as it guides us in an imaginative journey in which we gaze into the realm of infinity, where time and space are unlimited and boundless. Through this awareness, we may clearly experience that we are in the center of God. This is a wonderful awareness. Though best done in a sitting position, it can easily be adapted to do this when walking outside as well.

Assume a comfortable seated position and center yourself with the breath. Now imagine that you can travel back in time, fifty years. Now, imagine you can go back a hundred years, then a thousand years and then two thousand years and so forth.

Keep going farther and farther. Go as far as you can imagine. When you are unable to imagine "farther" as it is beyond your powers of imagination, know that you have touched infinity. Beyond infinity is *Ain Sof* (Limitless Light or what we also call God.) Know and respect that there is a realm in time, before even time was created, where your consciousness can not enter. Slowly bring your awareness back to the present moment. And take a few deep breaths to integrate what you received before proceeding.

Now allow your consciousness to travel into the future. Imagine the world in ten years, in a hundred years, in a thousand years, ten thousand years and so on. Know that as you go farther and farther, you will soon arrive at a place where you can conceive no further. Here you have touched what we call infinity. Infinity is a concept. Beyond infinity is *Ain Sof*. (God)

Now imagine you can travel in your consciousness through space. Begin by making yourself traveling upward, traveling through the heavens, past the stars, leaving this galaxy, traveling to other galaxies and going upward until you arrive a place where you cannot imagine any further. You have once again touched infinity in space. Beyond infinity is *Ain Sof*. Slowly bring your consciousness back to the present moment and pres- ent apace and take a few deep breaths.

Now imagine that you travel downward, into the earth, then again through space, going downward. Keep going through the galaxies until you can go no farther. For you have hit infinity. Beyond infinity is *Ain Sof*. Slowly return your awareness to the present moment, and the place where you are.

Now imagine that you can travel to eastward, journey past China, leaving the orbit of our earth once again into the galaxy, until you recognize that your imagination can take you no further. Again you touch a place that we call infinity. Beyond Infinity is *Ain Sof*.

Now travel westward, going past California, Hawaii, and out again into space, continuing as far as you can visualize, until you arrive once again at Infinity, Beyond infinity is *Ain Sof.*

Conclude this meditation by also imagining traveling north and south so you have journeyed in all directions.

Take a few deep breaths in the expanded awareness that you sit, stand and live in the middle of infinity in time and space. You are a point in this infinity. You are the center point. Every point, every person, everything that happens in life is the center point in infinity.

Repeat silently to yourself " I am the center point in *Ain Sof.* I am in the center of God." Internalize this awareness.

As you sit silently in this internalized awareness of infinity in time and space, allow the walls you have constructed that separate you from this expanded awareness to dissolve. Transcend your identification with the limited personality and ego self. You are not alone, or on your own. In this awareness, let go of painful emotions such as fear, anger, hurt and doubt.

Breathe these feelings out toward infinity. Give them to *Ain Sof* and let them dissolve in Divine Light. With every breath, let go and expand and connect to what is beyond you. Be permeated with this expanded awareness.

Continue to open to the awareness of infinity in both time and space. You are free to expand your consciousness as much as you like. You are free to contract your consciousness as much as you want. This is your choice.

Know that wherever you are, whether you go – to the highest place, to the deepest depths, you are always in the middle of infinity. There is no place else to go. There is no place to hide. *Ain Sof* encompasses all that was, is and will be in all places.

Just as you were born out of your mother's womb, imagine now that you are always in God's womb. This awareness is called the *Makom*, "The Place of the World" In this consciousness, feel yourself unconditionally loved and embraced.

God surrounds creation yet God is also with this world because this world is within God. Wherever you are, you are within God. Wherever you are, God is with you. God is within you.

3. KNOW YOURSELF AS THE SOUL MEDITATION

"The soul God created in you is pure. God created it, God blew it into you." (Morning prayers)

Take a few minutes to center yourself with inhaling long conscious deep breaths through the nostrils and exhaling through the mouth to let out tension and stress. Receive the inhalation with gratitude and hold it to your comfort level and then let go and allow yourself to go deeper inside.

Begin by focusing on your physical body. Scan the physical body and become compassionately aware of any pain and discomfort in the physical body. Be aware that your body is speaking to you in the form of sensations and pain. Then affirm to yourself that you may have sensations in your body but you are not your physical body. You are the soul who is inhabiting and witnessing the body. This physical body is a temporary residence for you. Affirm that you will honor and nourish this body temple for your soul for however long you are blessed to be embodied.

Now take a few moments to become compassionately aware of what emotions or feelings are present within you right now. There are no bad or good feelings. Allow yourself to be with what feelings are present for you. There may be sadness, anger, guilt, shame, jealousy. All your feelings are beautiful. Breathe and allow yourself to feel what is present for you without judgement. Then affirm that you have many emotions, but you are not the emotions or feelings you experience. You are the one who is aware of these emotions. You are the soul. You can welcome the wide expression of emotions without judgement, but with compassion, for these emotions reflect your human experience and not that of your soul essence.

Now become aware of the thoughts that travel through your mind. There may be thoughts of the past or the future, anxiety thoughts, judging thoughts or simply distracting thoughts that keep you from being present with yourself in the moment. Just be compassionately aware of these thoughts. Then affirm that you are not the thoughts of the mind trying to figure out life. You are the soul who is witnessing these thoughts.

You are the pure eternal and holy soul who is contained in this body time continuum having a human experience for a precious limited amount of time.

As we affirm greater identification with the witness, the soul, we can easily let go of limiting ideas of the ego mind. We naturally become more identified with the Divine for our soul is a part of God. Most likely, we will access glimpses of greater love and freedom in which to live our lives. Conclude this meditation by returning awareness to the breath, taking a few minutes to internalize and integrate what you opened to during meditation. When it is time for you, open your eyes.

CHAPTER 2

THE TRANSFORMATIONAL POWER OF HOLY TEARS

Most of us have, at some point, shed what can only be described as **holy tears**. These are moments when everything we cherish is stripped away. Whether through the loss of loved ones – or worse, their murder – the shattering of marriages, the onset of debilitating health challenges, the collapse of livelihoods, or the devastation of homes and communities by disaster or violence, our hearts break. The pain is immense. In these times, we cry for ourselves, we cry to God, and sometimes, we even cry for God, because God created this world, not for suffering, but to bestow love upon us.

There is no shame in such tears. The Torah itself instructs us to cry to God in times of pain and challenge. These tears arise not from weakness but from the depth of love and a firm belief in the goodness of God. The release of the tears triggered by challenge or loss is good. Holy tears break open the heart so we are better able to heal and receive blessing. **Do not deny yourself the gift of your own tears.** When we are in the midst of great pain, we all need to access the direct experience of God's love and Presence.

There is no replacement for it.

If and when we allow ourselves to call out to God and truly weep from the depth of our heart, we may enter a doorway into a most sacred space where God becomes more real than anything else in the world. In those holy moments, there is just you and God. When there are no more tears to cry, we eventually let go and surrender to the power greater than ourselves. Therein lies our freedom and protection.

Surrender is not resignation. It is liberation. It is actually liberating to let go of the illusion of one's self importance and the fantasy that we are in control of life. Accepting life as it is offers us entry into a holy state of humility and holy silence. In holy silence, we can hear the voice of our own soul and receive guidance from within our very being, beyond the need of the voice of the ego in its often manic efforts to control and understand reality. When we feel peaceful and uplifted, it is the wisdom of our own soul speaking to us.

With humility and acceptance, we shift from asking why we have suffered to asking how do we find meaning and purpose in our trials. In countless ways, we will then be inspired, empowered and miraculously find the strength to go forward and even bring more love into the world than we ever thought possible, a capacity born directly from the depths of our suffering. The trial we have experienced is our opportunity to triumph and transform pain into blessing.

AN ANCIENT TRADITION OF TRANSFORMATION

Crying holy tears is an ancient Jewish tradition, a spiritual gift to cry to God and for God. Such tears are precious. Like a sacred cleansing, they purify, strengthen, and open gates of blessing.

When we cry holy tears, we are walking in the sacred footsteps of many great beings and prophets. Our prophetess Chana is credited with showing us how to connect to God in a new and holy way when faced with a trial. Initially, when she poured out her heart, she was even mistaken for a drunken woman. 'She prayed to God weeping profusely and she vowed a vow. "O Lord of Hosts, if you will give Your maidservant a man child, I will dedicate him to God all the days of his life."'

Barren for many years, Chana advised her husband to marry another wife, Peninnah, so he could have children. Chana innocently believed Peninnah would graciously share in raising them. However, Peninnah was not gracious at all, relentlessly taunting Chana about her inability to conceive. Similar to the story of Hagar and Sarah, Peninnah also proclaimed that her easy childbirth meant she was more righteous than Chana.

Peninnah's betrayal was painful, but ultimately, it was a spiritual gift. Her cruelty inspired Chana to weep, plead, and bargain with God for a child in a way she had never done before. Though her cries were not answered immediately, she never gave up.

In time, her holy tears and prayers purified her and opened gates of blessing. It was Chana's destiny to give birth to the prophet Samuel, but she needed to grow spiritually before that could happen. Her worthiness became evident when she was guided to dedicate her son to be raised as a prophet upon his weaning. After Samuel's birth, Chana composed a song considered one of the most beautiful of all time. She was later blessed with many more children, while Peninnah buried some of hers.

Rachel and Leah, wives of Jacob, were also masters of holy tears. With her eyes tender from crying, Leah changed her destiny and birthed six tribes to become a mother of the Jewish people. Though not the beloved one in life, Leah is buried next to Jacob for eternity.

In the prophet Jeremiah, we read about the weeping of Mother Rachel for her children. In a midrash, Jacob explains the reason for burying his beloved wife Rachel on the road rather in Hebron in the plot where all the other matriarchs and patriarchs are buried. Jacob explains that there will be a time when the Jewish people will be exiled from the land promised to them. When they return they will pass Rachel's grave and she will beg for God's mercy for them. Thus the prophecy Jeremiah says, "A voice is heard in Ramah, lamentations and bitter crying. Rachel is weeping for her children.... (Jeremiah 31;15)

It has been said that Mother Rachel challenged God for all the pain and suffering the Jewish people have had to endure in exile and in the land of Israel as well. The midrash tells us that God's mercy was aroused and responded. "For you Rachel, I will bring Israel back to their place." For thousands of years, Rachel has waited alone, on the road, so that hundreds of thousands of women and men could come to her grave to weep and be comforted for the challenges experienced in life. To this day, thousands of people go to the grave of Mother Rachel each year. It has also been said that those who weep for the pain experienced by the Jewish people are spiritually rewarded. Their prayers will be answered.

Later on, our glorious King David became another well-known example of the power of holy tears. King David had a most challenging life from his very birth up until his last breath as king of Israel. Initially rising from his own pain, King David cried holy tears, which opened him to a divine flow of blessing and allowed him to compose the beautiful psalms. These psalms of King David have since uplifted millions of people of all faiths, with hundreds of thousands, possibly millions, reciting them daily.

The Gemara, the rabbinic commentary on the Bible, offers a relatively unknown story of Rabbi Elazar Ben Durdaya to illustrate the power of holy tears. It had been said that Elazar Ben Durdaya had sexual relations with every harlot in his vicinity. When he becomes aware of particularly infamous prostitute previously unknown to him, he travels a substantial distance and pays a great price to have her.

In the midst of sexual relations with her, she passes wind and says to him." Just as this wind will not return to its place, so too Elazar Ben Dordaya will not be accepted in repentance." Her words had a profound effect on him. He intensely searches for the means to repent and redeem himself. When all that he has known to help him has failed him, he places his head between his knees and cries loudly until his soul is lifted from his body. A Divine Voice declares "Rabbi Elazar Ben Dordaya is destined for life in the World to Come".

This story is told to remind us that weeping over our sins, by this we mean, the ways we have obstructed the flow of divine blessing in our lives, will open gates of blessing for us as well. Ibn Paquda also tells us in *Duties the Heart* that when a person has a broken heart, he attains a kind of humility that is the road to nearness with God. The worthiness to stand before God is then not far off. When we engage in sincere repentance with holy tears, we often will experience an immediate reward of inner peace, a sign that our tears have been wiped by the Creator.

Judaism has always honored the path of holy tears of individuals and of the community as a whole, even allocating several days for fasting and weeping over the pain the Jewish people have experienced. For thousands of years, Jews have cried over the destruction of the Holy Temples in Jerusalem, praying for restoration of the Holy Temple and for world peace. These commemorations affirm the belief that our tears are witnessed and make a difference.

Upon witnessing and learning that the Jewish people have been weeping for the destruction of their Holy Temples for a thousand years or more, the emperor Napoleon stated that the Jewish people will undoubtedly return to Jerusalem and have their holy temple rebuilt. In 1948 when the modern state of Israel was established, we have seen for ourselves, that tears and prayers have been answered and Jewish prophecy has been fulfilled. We therefore can trust that prophecies will be continued to be fulfilled in the future as well.

Unlike several other religions which may also believe in the existence of a Supreme Creator, Judaism has always emphasized the dynamic relationship individuals can have with the Creator. Judaism affirms that God answers the cries of a sincere heart. Our tears and prayers make a difference, even if we do not experience immediate confirmation that they are heard or working. Tears from the heart are holy and redemptive, not just for ourselves, but redemptive to the world as well.

Tears of self pity and feelings of victimhood, however, in themselves do not open gates of blessing. These tears are draining, leaving us exhausted, depressed and sorry for ourselves. Yet whenever we cry, when we can become mindful that God is listening, present for us, we have an opportunity to cry to God and cry for God. Our tears can be converted to holy tears. Holy tears transform our lives into blessing.

Rabbi Nachman of Breslov spoke often about the preciousness of a broken heart. A broken heart actually allows Divine light to enter a person. If a person is too sure of himself, too proud, too angry, there is a wall around his heart that prevents God's light and love from entering.

Many of us unfortunately received messages that it is not appropriate or good to cry in public, to others and even to ourselves. We have all heard variations of the message that "You should not feel the way you do." Or "Toughen up and be strong."

Because we are often afraid of our own sadness and feelings of helplessness, as well of that of other people, we do not cry privately, we do not cry to God or cry to other people when it would be bonding to do so. This is unfortunate because the release of tears is healing. We are not weak or bad because we have certain feelings and we cry.

Crying to a person who can truly listen and crying with someone as you hold each other offers a most powerful release. These tears are healing and restorative. When was the last time you hugged someone who was crying or were hugged when you were crying? Many people even go to therapists primarily to open their hearts and cry.

The Baal Shem Tov reminds us "in the king's palace there are many gates and doors that lead to many halls and chambers... There is a master key that opens all the doors. And can open the innermost chambers of the Divine palace. The master key is the tears of a broken heart." (*Positivity Bias* by Rabbi Mendel Kalmenson)

INSPIRATIONAL STORIES OF HOLY TEARS

The following are accounts of parents who lost a beloved child along with one story about the loss of a mother. Our hearts may break when we read their stories. Even as they wrestle with faith, these stories also inspire us. Their pain was immense, yet they went on to be of greater service to others than they might have done otherwise because of their losses.

In these stories we witness the power of holy tears to God and how each person was inspired to grow in faith. Prayers were answered, just not in the way they might necessarily wanted them to be.

We do not have to have experienced this kind of trial to identify with these stories and be inspired by them. Yet, there will be many people who read this book who have also experienced a painful loss, so it is my hope that these stories will be particularly meaningful and helpful to them.

If you have experienced a loss, may you be comforted for your loss. You are not alone. If it is possible for you, recite the special Kaddish prayer for mourners for that will bring consolation to you.

LOSS OF AN INFANT HELPS ESTABLISH WORLD WIDE COMMUNITY FOR BURYING PEOPLE WITH LOVE AND DIGNITY.

Elissa Felder

Excerpts from Felder's book *One Life to Another*, printed with permission about the death of her three month old son named Sam.

"Immediately after Sam died, I experienced a tailspin of out of control grief, so raw and wild that I could see no end in sight. My world went very dark. I was lost. It was though I had hit an insurmountable wall. I had no preparation for this moment, no guidebook to consult. I had no idea how to keep living. I really could not imagine a world without Sam in it. I wept bitterly for my baby, for all my hopes and dreams that were dashed so early on and for the pain of losing a part of myself, I did not know to pick myself up. There was just so much pain: physical, emotional and theological. I couldn't sleep. I couldn't function.

When I felt dragged down by grief, I felt badly that I was not moving forward. I really wanted to be better. When I was feeling stronger I felt guilty that I was leaving Sam behind. It became clear that I was not functioning well and needed professional help. I started seeing a skilled grief therapist, who, among other things, encouraged me to talk to Sam. Session after session, I spoke to Sam.

In addition, I looked 'up' – I needed God to bring me strength and comfort. The same God who had blessed us with Sam was the same God who took Sam away from us. My prayers had not been answered the way I had wanted, but never for a moment did I believe that they had not been heard. So I cried to God and I also believe that God was crying with me… I held on to God and the belief that God would somehow help me survive and thrive.

I cried and cried bitter tears of grief, of loss, of sadness until, one day, I just could not cry any more. I was all dried up. I felt exhausted and on some level 'done' with crying.

My husband and I were blessed to have people in our lives who could be with us as we walked into an unchartered dark tunnel and continued to hold our hands and stand alongside us for as long as we needed.

At some point after Sam died, a dear friend, attempting to offer some comfort, shared with me that she and a few other ladies had formed a *Chevra Kadisha* (a holy society) from our synagogue and that they had lovingly prepared him for his burial. I had never thought about the work of the *Chevra Kadisha* until then.

I wanted to understand this tradition more and I have subsequently learned so much about the practice and what they do. I learned that the *Chevra Kadisha* are kind and loving and do their preparations with great dignity and respect for the dead. Through their care, the soul of the deceased is elevated to higher levels in the spiritual worlds.

My friends who knew Sam in life had brought their love for him into the way that they took care of him in death. They got him ready to be planted in the earth the next day. They said the traditional prayers and thought holy thoughts to bring about sacred purification. Knowing all this was supremely comforting."

Quite miraculously, we adopted a baby girl on the anniversary of Sam's death one year later. To me, this was God winking, saying, "I love you." There is the baby that you need and who needs you. Be a family, raise her, nurture her, and love her.

Then we were blessed with another healthy baby born a few months after the adoption. Subsequently, we were blessed with another baby 14 months later. Three children in less than 2 years!

"Because I saw and so appreciated the holiness of the rituals performed for Sam by the *Chevra Kadisha,* I was motivated to participate in this mitzvah myself. My involvement in *Chevra*

Kadisha has become an anchor for me. It is a practice that is both grounding and humbling. It forces one to face one's own mortality on an ongoing basis and gives a heightened appreciation for the gift of life."

"In grieving for Sam I believe I was able to achieve greater levels of sensitivity and compassion for others experiencing loss, than I would have otherwise. I found a capacity for deeper soul connections. I certainly believe myself to have become more empathetic than I was before. Sam challenged me to grow and mature in ways I otherwise would not have."

"Over time, I became an active leader and teacher for an international Jewish organization called CORE. In this role I connect, advocate for, support and inspire female volunteers of *Chevra Kadisha* societies all over the world. In this work I find great meaning and feel that I am able to bring knowledge and comfort to many."

Elissa Felder has written a book called, *"From One Life to the Next Life: The Sacred Passage after Death,"* printed in 2024 and speaks widely to audiences on the topics of grief, loss, death, afterlife and the work of the *Chevra Kadisha*.

LOSS OF A CHILD TO TERRORISM INSPIRED A FOUNDATION OFFERING COUNSELING AND PROGRAMS FOR WOMEN AND CHILDREN WHO ALSO SUFFERED LOSS OF LOVED ONES THROUGH TERRORISM

Sherry Mandell

Excerpts from Sherry Mandell's important book *The Blessing of a Broken Heart,* used with her permission.

"Koby was my first child, the child who taught me to be a mother. I could have stayed in bed the rest of my life mourning him, I could have remained broken, resenting my life, my lot. But there is something in my heart refuses to be broken, no matter how intense the pain, something that moves toward the light... I have not come to this belief in the soul easily. Often the belief flies away. But that is that nature of my faith. When God created the heaven and the earth, the Bible states "the spirit of God hovered over the face of the water." Rashi compares the spirit of God to a dove hovering over its nest. God's presence is like that too. It does not force you to recognize it. But it is something that covers you, and then alights; something that does not stay put, but flies off just when you may be looking for it.

Since Koby's death, the spirit of God has hovered over me, flickering and returning. There have been moments of revelation, moments when I felt God was touching me, pointing me, moving me, hugging me. They are inner moments, windows that open so that I can view my son's death in a different light. I know that my broken heart will never be the same. I will always long for Koby and feel the pain of his absence. But it is possible to build a new heart.

Last summer, after going to the camp with other children who lost siblings or parents to terror, my daughter Eliana explained to me why she liked camp so much. "It is like we touched each others hearts," she said. "We put our hearts together and we made a new heart." When we touch broken hearts together, a new heart emerges, one that is more open and compassionate, able to touch others, a heart that seeks God. That is the blessing of a broken heart.

People ask me, How are you? Now it is not one that I cannot answer. There is no okay. Suffering has thrust me into a world where there is no okay. Each moment is a miracle and an agony. A miracle that the world exists in all its glory. An agony that this world is one of suffering and pain. Jewish tradition says that each person is a world. I have lost a whole world.

Some people tell me to be strong. They want me to reassure them that there is hope in the world. Keep going so that we can see that life is possible after your child is dead. But what they mean by being strong is not what I mean. I believe that being strong means feeling pain, letting my body mourn, letting my mind mourn, letting my soul mourn, entering the pain and not fleeing it.

A mother who loses a child is bad. I am a guilty mother. I am a bad mother, one who has lost all she was supposed to protect and cherish. There is the pain and then there is the guilt. You can recover from the pain, but guilt can eat you every day like acid.

"I struggle to hold on to my belief in the justice of God's world. I struggle to believe that God is good. I cannot believe otherwise. What occurs to us is not an accident. How could it be-when the whole world is so clearly orchestrated- that we, too are not also part of the symphony?

"How could God let my son be killed so brutally? I believe the Talmud when it says that God suffers as we suffer. God is in pain when people are in pain. Many people give up belief in God because of the suffering they witness. But I refuse to believe in God's cruelty. I believe that what we view as cruelty may one day, in face, be revealed as part of God's plan.

Everything, even Koby's death, has a purpose. Seth and I know that we have to do something to keep Koby's spirit alive. We cannot let his spirit die. We decide to do something that Koby would enjoy. We decide to make a summer camp for children in Israel whose mothers and fathers and sisters and brothers have been killed by terror. Over five hundred kids join us and they are happy to be together. We have sports, and trips, and art and music and movement therapy, but the real pleasure is for the kids not to be alone.

We take mothers for workshops. I think it is wonderful to take away bereaved mothers and let us be together and give us a chance to be away from our families and take care of their own feelings. "It is a feeling of being 'normal" with what is so abnormal." The follow up programs for mothers are monthly meetings.

We run healing retreats for women. One mother shared that after losing two children in a terrorist attack, she felt she could not go on, she felt so guilty, so bad. She was ready to kill herself but then she realized that she had to accept God's decree, she had to talk her suffering and live with it. These projects help me. I need to take the love and support I have been given, the angels around me and share them with other mothers and families. I have been blessed with support and I bring that support to other families."

Update as of 2025. Sherri Mandell is now a grandmother, busy with her family. She has a new memoir coming out in 2026, "From Mac to Matbucha: My Life in Recipes" about her transformation from a feminist secular woman to a religious (feminist) Israeli. She also writes children's picture books. Her latest book is "Shabbat Shalom, The Trucks Come Home." Her daughter, Eliana, is now the director of the Koby Mandel Center.

LOSS OF SON TO SUICIDE: A SOUL MISSION BORN OUT OF GRIEF

Brian Halloran

A local policeman knocked on my door. It was a Tuesday evening, approximately 8:00 PM, so this visit was quite out of the norm. I often wish I had never answered the door because that night I was informed that my son Brian, 19 years old had lost his battle to depression and died by suicide while a freshman at the University of South Carolina. Holy Crap! My world stopped at that moment and has been completely altered to this very day! What am I going to do?

Brian was/is my middle son and is so precious to me, as are all my three boys. It broke my heart when he came to us two years prior, in the middle of the night, to finally tell us that he wasn't feeling well, he felt off, sad and unhappy. Immediately sadness and panic ripped through my veins, afraid of what I was hearing and unsure how to effectively address this major issue. Thus, we set on the path to find the best psychiatrist and counselor for Brian. Alas, this is not an easy task. Who takes insurance? Who is accepting new patients? The best clinicians, the ones that you are the most often referred to, are fully booked and inaccessible.

On that January night I had to face Brian's death time and time again as I had to tell my wife, who was upstairs at the time and my younger son, who was downstairs on the treadmill. That was not the end, at 4:00 AM I drove to Saratoga Springs, Skidmore College to tell me oldest son that his brother died!!!!!!! The details surrounding these exchanges are blurry and too painful to remember or even share. The car ride home was filled with hysterical tears to the point that it was difficult to drive, but we needed to get home to the rest of the family. By the time we arrived, a group of friends were already there to support us. My son went up to his room to be alone. OMG, what has happened to us?

This was the most challenging time of my life and remains so to this day. I love my son. I miss my son. I want him back. I wish I was able to help him more. Brian's passing made me question my faith in God and my religious beliefs. How could my God allow this beautiful boy, my son to suffer to the extent that he felt the need to end his life? Well.... how do we explain that?

Overtime and with some counseling I began to view things differently. Maybe God allowed Brian to leave so that he would not have to endure a life of pain. Maybe things could have gotten worse for Brian and us. Other families suffer tremendous tragedies, why should we be spared – should it just happen to someone else? All questions that will never be answered. Although my mindset had shifted somewhat, my challenges with religion remained. I no longer attend mass, while I did so sporadically all my life. I spoke/speak to God in a different way now, a more personal way. There were both positives and negatives to this new relationship with God.

In the days following Brian's passing, I was in a fog. At the wake, we welcomed over 1,000 caring souls that took time to share their condolences followed by a large funeral mass and burial the next day. Our family invited attendees to lunch after the burial, we hosted approximately 250 family and friends. It was after the burial that things started to get much harder for me. I was lost, beaten down – a man living in deep grief and there was nothing I could do to bring my SON BACK! There was no more future with Brian as a part of our family. There would be no marriage, grandkids, etc. Our family, while reduced by one, felt like it had been shattered in pieces, left as a fragment of what we were. It was at this time that we began to consider starting a foundation around youth wellness and suicide prevention. We needed a way to direct and harness our pain and energy into something more positive. We as a family, decided that others should not have to endure such loss and pain. This can be prevented, people can be helped.

Hence, the launch of Break the Hold (BTH initials are Brian's initials – Brian Thomas Halloran). BTH began as an organization supporting youth wellness and suicide prevention by hosting awareness events and providing resources to the community. Our aim is to Break the Hold on mental illness and the stigma surrounding it. Over time, Break the Hold has morphed into a leading provider of SEL programming in Westchester County, N.Y. After much consultation, we unanimously decided to base our program on DBT Steps-A, skills training for emotional problem solving for adolescents. Our program, BTH 360 delivers this evidence-based instruction universally to students in schools in Westchester County and beyond, currently serving 9 school districts and more than 4,000 students. BTH 360 is expanding aggressively and has begun to collaborate with NY Presbyterian Hospital to more effectively measure outcomes to enable the creation of a state-wide model. Our goal is to be state-wide (min. 75% of school districts) by 2030, followed by the launch of a national model.

BTH 360 is based on the belief that EDUCATION and EARLY INTERVENTION can reverse decades long trends in youth mental health. Just consider for a moment, the next generation will be armed with information regarding their mental health journey and will learn to develop skills to support their emotional well-being. This will lead to increased peer support and early intervention for those in need. This, in turn, will produce improved outcomes and the avoidance of life-long illness.

BTH 360 is delivered at no-cost to the school district. The model works in this manner:

- Year 1 – BTH sponsors a certified specialist to deliver the instruction in health classes to all students. 10-15 sessions an academic year.

- Year 1 – BTH sponsors the certification/training of 2-3 teachers in said school district.
- Year 2 – Certified teachers assume the instruction of the curriculum ensuring the no-cost, evidence-based instruction is permanently embedded in the health curriculum impacting generations to come.
- Year 2 – BTH moves resources/instructors to a new school district to continue our expansion.

Life events often shape us into the person that we eventually become, for the good and bad. However much of it depends on us. How do we react to this trauma? How do we live the rest of our lives? The absolute blessing of such a loss is that we now know the secret to life. The understanding that life does not last forever and can be gone in a flash. Do not take the beauty of life for granted. Do not live under some false pretense that all is good in the world. Life comes with much pain and sorrow, and it is all a blessing. It makes us who we are, what we become, how we spend our time here on earth. Pain allows us to really feel happiness and loss allows us to truly feel love. These blessings do not come easy.

Much of my early years as a father were spent chasing an economic dream, which proved to be exhausting and not very rewarding. My job was to care for my family, but my focus was a little narrow. Now, with the blessing of feeling this pain, I realize that what matters most is what I can do for others and the love I can give my family. Given our short time on this planet, it is what we do for others that will be the true testament to our life. Empathy and caring can go a long way in helping others that are struggling. Our world is all about connection – that's what makes us human. It is time to stand together and fight for mental health and suicide prevention, especially for our youth.

I have learned that I cannot control much of what happens

in my life. So, for that I must trust in God that all things happen for a reason and that Brian's 19 years on earth were meant to be the driving force in helping so many other young people. Brian is saving lives in his departure. He is the energy, focus and determination behind our efforts to help others through Break the Hold. Brian is still "doing it!" Let's Go, Brian!! Love Ya!

Today, my focus is to support my family in any way that I can, and to be there for other families. I stand tall in the wake of my son's tragedy, and I work hard to represent Brian in a way that would make him proud. My mission is to ensure that the next generations grow up with a better chance, a better understanding of their mental health, skills to help regulate emotions, and the understanding that if intervention is needed, earlier is better. Life is great, it is important that we live it to the fullest. The world is a better place with you in it.

I am a loving father of 3 boys; I am a boy dad! This is the greatest gift I have in life, being a father to three great individuals. It was my dream, and I got to live it. Even with the trauma our family has suffered, we continue to walk a Godly path in the service of others. We can truly help as we have been blessed with the ultimate pain and loss of a young family member, my boy, Bri-Bri! Our family will continue to grow and hopefully thrive as we proceed through our time on this planet. We will work to stop youth suicide, with zero being the goal. Until we meet again, Brian.

Brian Halloran, Dad, Founder and Executive Director of **Break the Hold**,(BTH) Suicide Prevention through education raising awareness, formed in memory of son Brian.

P.S. Each day in the U.S, there is an average of over 3,470 suicide attempts by young people in grades 9-12. Four of five teens who attempt suicide have given clear warning signs. We can't measure the impact of BTH. It likely has saved many lives of teens. For more information and to be educated about suicide prevention, contact **bthbreakthehold.org**

DEATH OF MOTHER LED TO CREATION OF EVENING MINYAN AND COMMUNITY FOR THOSE EXPERIENCING LOSS OF LOVED ONES AND PHYSICAL CHALLENGES.

Geela Rayzel Raphael

In December 2020, at the height of the COVID shutdowns, my beloved mother, Natalie Robinson z'l, (Nechama Leah bat Elke) was locked inside a senior care facility in Atlanta, Ga. No visitors were allowed. I could see her only through a window, speaking words of love muffled by glass and confusion. It was excruciating. As I stood there saying goodbye, I knew; deep in my bones, that this might be the last time I would ever see her.

I drove from Atlanta to Florida to stay in her condo, to sit in the sunshine, to begin the painful task of sorting through her belongings. A few days later, the call came: If you want to see her, come now. I flew back immediately. My brothers and I had decided – no more interventions, we need to let her go. I spent three days at her bedside as she transitioned to another plane of existence.

My relationship with my mother had not always been easy. In my early years, it was often contentious. But time softened us. We grew into a genuine friendship, one built on affection, humor, and mutual respect. Being at her side during those final days was a profound gift. I sang to her. I told her stories. I whispered what I would say about her in her eulogy. I did my best to stay fully present to her dying, to accompany her with love.

I left the hospital on December 30th.

I was scheduled to produce and host an online New Year's Eve gala, a virtual gathering of artists and performers. I leaned close to my mother and pleaded, half-joking and half-desperate, Please don't die yet. I need to do that program. She didn't listen. She died in the wee hours of the morning of Dec 31.

Because I had been exposed to COVID, no one wanted to be near me. I checked into a hotel alone on the very day my mother died. That night, the show went on. I hosted a Zoom gala, and told the community what had happened, and was held – truly held – by their presence. Their care carried me through the funeral and the days that followed. My husband, Simcha, flew to meet me for the funeral, but we were both isolated from the family *Shiva*. When he left, I was once again largely alone. I knew then that I needed to build something intentional to support myself in the weeks and months ahead.

Jewish tradition is deeply wise in its approach to death and mourning. The first week after a death is *Shiva,* when the mourner stays home, sits low to the ground, and allows others to come; bringing food, stories, and companionship to soften the sharp edges of acute grief. The first thirty days, *Shloshim,* hold a different quality: grief is still fresh, but beginning to shift. And then there is the practice of saying *Kaddish,* the holy prayer that praises God, for eleven months – a sacred rhythm that helps the soul rise while allowing the living to remember, metabolize grief, and mark time until the unveiling of the tombstone. I knew I needed community to survive this eleven months.

During the first week after my mother's death, my brothers – each in different cities, and I convened an online *Shiva*. Each night a different rabbinical colleague and friend – hosted the gathering. We prayed, sang, and told stories about my mother. I was physically alone in Florida with only my husband, yet spiritually surrounded.

When *Shiva* ended, I realized I still needed to be held through the full thirty days of *Shloshim*. My husband would soon return to Philadelphia, and I did not want the circle to dissolve. I invited colleagues and friends to continue leading nightly online services.

For a month, every evening, I showed up to an hour of prayer, meditation, song, and remembrance; each night guided by someone I loved and trusted.

When it was time to return to my home in Philadelphia, I knew the support could not stop. I began organizing a nightly prayer minyan at 9:00 p.m. so I could say Kaddish. Because it was COVID, many others were also grieving. People joined me – not only to mourn my mother, but to hold their own losses. We scraped together the ten people needed for a minyan, sometimes by twisting arms and sending last minute texts. And yes, people showed up.

Over time, the gathering grew. More leaders volunteered. The prayers took on many forms; different melodies, meditations, styles, and spiritual languages. What began as a lifeline for my grief became a rich, evolving tapestry of communal prayer. I sustained the practice for my full year of Kaddish.

At the end of that year, I realized what an extraordinary gift this had been. On the anniversary of my mother's death – New Year's Eve – I announced that the minyan – now called the Nechama Minyan – named after my mother and meaning "comfort" would continue. People signed up. And now, five years later, what emerged from grief has become something far larger than I could have imagined.

We have built a community that prays together every night. I have met people I never would have known otherwise. My own prayer vocabulary has expanded beyond measure. Over time, the minyan has taken on a life of its own. Devoted participants hold the space nightly; whether or not they are personally saying Kaddish, so others can arrive and be held in a loving virtual embrace. We added a D'var Torah – a short teaching – each night. It is sometimes a deep dive into the weekly portion, sometimes a simple blessing offered from the heart.

We also added prayers for healing. People now come simply to hear their names spoken aloud, lifted in prayer. Our motto is:

"We will pray for you". We pray for those with chronic illness, long COVID, pain, homelessness, fear, and despair. We have seen profound suffering in that Zoom room, and we have discovered that our emotional container is strong enough to hold it.

Some of the people who first met as small squares on a screen now meet in person, visiting each other as they travel. We have welcomed participants from Hawaii, Israel, Kazakhstan, Canada, South America, Mexico, and across the United States. The hour – 9:00 to 10:00 p.m. Eastern – allows East and West Coast, and even other time zones, to meet in sacred time.

The minyan is entirely volunteer-run. After the service, devoted Zoom *gabbai'im,* our logistics team manage the room; welcoming newcomers, muting noise, tending to frayed emotions, and gently supporting those stepping into leadership.

What I have witnessed humbles me. We have held hands through divorces, traumatic grief, and loss. We have prayed with people from hospital bedsides, through brain surgery, pacemaker scares, and moments of real vulnerability. We have become a healing community – even from within the small frame of a Zoom room.

We have held space for prayer for ourselves, for our country, for Israel, for Palestinians, for peace. We have gathered in grief after mass shootings. We have marked minor holidays together. (We do not meet on Friday nights or major Jewish holidays)

If my mother could have imagined that her death would spark a community of souls spanning time zones and continents; a circle devoted to compassion, witnessing, prayer, and listening I believe she would be flooded with astonished delight.

Her death was an ending. But it was also, unmistakably, a beginning. Something beautiful has grown between the cracks in my heart.

Rabbi Geela Rayzel Raphael, an award-winning singer/songwriter and Jewish teacher. She offers life cycle events and trips to places of Jewish interest all over the world. Her Nechama Minyan remains available to all. www.shechinah.com

CHAPTER 3

THE GIFT OF CHALLENGE

When faced with a trial, we will all do our best to cope, heal, and survive. Yet, we often find that the final outcome is not in our hands. Two people with the same cancer diagnosis may have completely different outcomes. One person survives a car accident; another does not. One person is targeted for murder. Instead, another person is murdered in his place. This randomness can feel deeply unfair and leave us questioning why.

This is where the wisdom of classic spiritual teachings, such as those found in the Jewish classic *Duties of the Heart* by Ibn Paquda, offers a transformative perspective. The core teaching is this: nothing can happen to us – neither harm nor benefit – without the permission of God. Our efforts matter and are important, but the ultimate outcome is part of a Divine plan. Ibn Paquda's lesson is a profound one:

> *"No one can increase what God decreed shall be less. Nor decrease what God decreed shall be more. None can cause an event to happen earlier than God decreed it shall happen later."*

It is helpful to repeat and meditate upon these verses for they have the potential to liberate us from the burden of self-blame as well as the blaming of others for our trials. This teaching also reminds us to not take credit or accept praise for our good deeds and successes as well.

As we come to better accept that God is in charge of life, we awaken to a deeper truth that our life experiences are not random. Everything is purposeful, even if it was painful. God is in charge. We all have what God intends us to have at this time. We all have what we are capable of receiving. What has happened in our life is part of our soul journey in the way and timing it was meant to unfold. What has happened to others is part of their soul journey as well. Everything that has happened in life is a learning opportunity designed to take us deeper and forward.

It often takes a challenge or a trial to wake us to experience that who we are as human beings in life is much more than just physical. We are multi-dimensional beings. We are not limited to what has taken place or is taking place in our lives on a physical level. This expanded awareness of ourselves is in itself a profound blessing. When we experience ourselves as multi-dimensional beings, we know that life is much deeper than it first appears to be.

We each have a soul shining within us, no matter what is happening in our bodies, in our thoughts and in our emotions. This soul is our truest essence. It is who we were before we entered into this incarnation and who we will be when we depart from it. It is therefore incumbent upon each of us to access and nurture our own soul and deepen our experience of the most important relationship we can have in our lives: that is, the relationship we can have with the Creator, the Infinite, Loving and Intelligent Being with so many names, but is one true essence that we call God in this book.

Our soul did not come into this world for money, possessions, or fame; it came for a deeper connection with God. Our soul came to reveal and share the light and love of God in this physical world. Our pain and challenge is a springboard to deepen our relationship to God, to fulfill our very own soul purpose. Only when we are fulfilling our soul purpose, will we feel fulfilled and even peaceful, regardless of what is happening in our lives. It therefore behooves us to learn to listen to the voice of our own soul and receive her guidance.

Countless people can testify that they grew in love, compassion, and spiritual depth through their most difficult experiences. Many go on to do something extraordinary – something they would not have done otherwise. They turn their pain into a blessing for themselves and others. I have seen this firsthand many times in my therapy practice. People come to therapy in pain, and when successful, they learn not only to cope but to transform that pain into a gateway to a more meaningful life.

I once worked for two years with a couple whose son murdered his new bride. They were on the brink of divorce and unemployment, riddled with blame, depression, and anxiety. Their son was on death row! Through therapy, they learned to communicate with love and respect, but something even more powerful happened: they began to pray. They recited psalms daily, began to attend church, and found a supportive community. As their faith deepened, their marriage improved, and they became more compassionate, empowered and centered people. This unimaginable tragedy ultimately led them to an authentic, loving relationship with God and membership in a loving expanded spiritual religious community. They were now living a more purposeful life than they ever could have imagined previously. Most likely, many people witnessing their transformation were inspired.

For many of us, suffering similarly becomes a gift only when it brings us to our knees, humbling us, calling out for a deeper connection and alignment with God. Some of us have to be broken through suffering and extreme adversity to call out to God, to experience God, and ultimately to surrender to God. The greater the affliction often elicits a greater surrender.

This surrender to God is not about giving up; it is the letting go of what no longer serves or limits us. It is the letting go of what is no longer true nor sustainable and opening to that which is true and empowering. When we are down on our knees-literally or symbolically- in an authentic way, we find that God lifts us up. Surrender gifts us access to a new, more conscious, heart centered and expanded way of life. In the privacy of our homes, we need to give ourselves time to stand before God, and even get down on our knees if we feel guided to do so. Wherever we are, we can open our heart and experience ourselves directly before the Divine Presence.

It is elevating but not necessary to travel to holy places to experience God. We can stand at the holiest of sites and feel absolutely nothing if our hearts are closed. We can be in our own home and feel the Divine Presence in the most intense and holiest of ways. As the Baal Shem Tov told us, people are where their thoughts are.

When we call out to God, when we connect with God, when we surrender to God, we find love and blessings even in the darkest moments. God wipes our tears. We can be in the most challenging of circumstances – in a war zone, in a tunnel in Gaza as a hostage or facing a terminal illness, and we can still feel God's love in a way we never experienced before.

Conversely, suffering remains a great burden when we resist the presence of God in our lives. If we are stubborn and blame circumstances, others and even ourselves for our suffering, our heart will harden like Pharaoh's in the ancient biblical story. We become unable to receive blessings from our trials and continue to suffer, becoming increasingly disempowered.

We are given a choice. We either see God's hand in our experiences or we do not. As the Vorker Rebbe once taught, we don't choose what happens to us, but we can choose how we view and experience it.

While we face many external challenges, the greatest enemy is often our own negative inclination, according to Ibn Paquda. **The true source of our suffering is not what happens to us, but how we interpret it.** The negative inclination tells us that life is random, there is no God, we are victims and our lives have no purpose nor hope. This inner voice robs us of joy and connection. When we overcome this negative inclination, we open ourselves to the flow of blessings and feel gratitude, no matter what is happening.

Gratitude is a powerful weapon to defeat the evil inclination. Gratitude empowers us to live with greater reciprocity and divine connection. When we are grateful, we let go of reactivity and become receptive to life, to ourselves, to God. Simply stated, when we are grateful, we are essentially saying yes to God, yes to life, yes to ourselves, and yes to living each moment. The practice of gratitude changes our life.

Through practicing gratitude, we come to embody the holy attributes of humility and trust. Gratitude enables us to release fear or anger, and live with greater faith and trust. We accept what life has unfolded for us as our highest good because God is in charge. This may be challenging in the midst of trials but there is always something to be grateful for, even if it is only for our breath. Our very breath is an awesome gift of love. Being alive is a blessing. When we practice gratitude, we draw to us more reasons to be grateful in life.

In his book of teachings, *HaSulam; The Ladder*. Rabbi Yehuda Leib Ashlag may have gone a little deeper in telling us that when something happens to oneself or a loved one, whatever it is, we should think that God did it. Receive everything with love and know that God does everything for the good of a person. Believe that this is so, even though your mind may say it cannot be so.

When we suffer, we always have a choice. We may cleave to the negativity of the suffering and continue to suffer. Or, we can cleave to the one who produced the negativity; that is, God. By acknowledging and cleaving to God in the midst of suffering, we will be delivered out of negativity. Rabbi Ashlag said something like "When we are not blinded by our self love, we can see through the eyes of God, and know the secrets of why something happened in life and we would not suffer". Seeing ourselves as we imagine how God sees us, knowing that God desires our highest good. This itself is a meditation.

Even with all these teachings, we can still have questions. "Where is God"? Where is justice?" Do I deserve this pain? Why has this happened? My teacher Reb Shlomo Carlebach of blessed memory used to say, "What is the matter with a question? A question can be very deep. Questions do not always require answers. Some questions do not have answers".

Our questions are often much deeper than any answers we attempt to explain or rationalize our pain. It is good to be with one's questions. Let your questions break open your heart, humble you, and bring holy tears to connect you with the Creator.

Through suffering, we learn firsthand that life is not simple. Life is deep and mysterious. God is deep. God is real. When we are in pain, we realize that we do not control life, nor do we control God. Pain enables us to see through illusions, access the depths of life and open to the reality of God in a much deeper way. When we do this, we are given strength.

SUPPORTIVE AFFIRMATION & MEDITATION PRACTICES

SUMMARY AFFIRMATION

Repeat and meditate on this affirmation as much as desired. Allow the words to enter the heart so they are an expression of what is true for you.

When I accept that God is in charge of my life, I accept that I have been gifted with experiences tailored to my soul's mission. My challenges have a divine purpose and offer me my greatest learning opportunities. I know that whatever happens in my life is ultimately good, even if it does not feel good at the time. My connection to God is my lifeline. I accept myself and my life experiences as part of my journey as a human being. When I do this, I experience inner peace and love. I know that I am blessed.

PSALM #23 TO BE REPEATED FREQUENTLY

Adonai (God) is my shepherd, I shall not want. In lush pastures God makes me lie beside tranquil waters he leads me. God restores my soul. God directs me in paths of righteousness for the sake of His Name.

Though I walk in the valley of the shadow of death. I will fear no evil for You are with me. Your rod and your staff comfort me. You prepare a table for me in the full presence of my enemies. You anointed my head with oil. My cup overflows.

May only good and kindness pursue me all the days of my life. And I shall dwell in the house of Adonai for long days.

YOU ARE NOT ALONE MEDITATION

Visualize a spiritual, emotional and material goal or vision for yourself at this time in your life. Select an image to symbolize this goal. Imagine that in front of you lies a long straight clear path to the top of the hill. Place your symbol on the top of the hill. As you travel this path, you may hear voices of other people or within yourself telling you how difficult it will be to reach the top of the hill. This is an opportunity to recognize the internal resistances, fears, and external opposition to your going forward in your life. You may want to take time to journal what you experience.

Now repeat this visualization. But this time as you travel up the path, you see and hear people who are encouraging and supporting you to go forward and reach the top of the hill. Imagine people you know as well as people you do not know. Imagine people from the Bible cheering you, applauding you for each step you take forward. Moses, Abraham, Sarah, Rebecca, and more are rooting for you. Your parents, your ancestors, your friends and family are rooting for you. You are not alone.

Most importantly, now open to the experience that you are divinely supported to climb the hill and reach the summit. Breathe and know that God is supporting and empowering you to go forward to reach the top of the hill or what you may experience as a mountain. Continue to take steps forward. You can do this.

Now, take a leap. Visualize that you have reached the top of the hill and absorb all the wonderful feelings of accomplishment and victory of this experience reaching the top of the hill. You were able to reach your goal. Take time to journal and record what this experience is for you.

THREE AFFIRMATIONS TO CHANGE YOUR ENERGY AND LIFE

These three affirmations help us to heal and go forward in the midst of challenge. After you have done breathing to center yourself, repeat to yourself silently or out loud and then meditate on the following affirmations: Repeat these mantras for five or ten minutes with the breath. They will change your energy.

God is the power that illuminates darkness. I came to this world to radiate light. When I am attached to God, I radiate light. Darkness has no hold on me I came here to radiate light. This is the truth. I do not have to try to change others, the light I radiate will change them, when they are ready to change.

God is the power that erases fear. Fear comes from a sense of separation. I am here on my own. When I experience God's love, I know that I am loved. I am not afraid of life. I can relinquish fear. God's love fills and sustains me. This is the truth. God is the power of love.

God is the power that enables me to overcome addiction, challenge and affliction. This is the truth. When I align with the power of God, I am empowered to overcome addiction, challenge and affliction.

There is no power greater than that of God.

Allow these mantras to permeate you deeply for they are the truth. God is supporting you. God is loving you, God is protecting you.

Please see the video on these three affirmations on my You Tube channel

INSPIRATIONAL STORIES: OVERCOMING LIFE CHALLENGES

In this chapter, we read the stories of people overcoming different personal challenges in unique ways. What unites these stories is that these people, not only overcame their challenges, they did something to help others that they would not have done otherwise. Several even became empowered to do great things. We can't measure the positive impact that their lives have had on others due to the trials they faced.

I want to thank all the contributors for sharing themselves so authentically and deeply for this book. When we share our stories with others or we make a heart connection with those who share their stories with us, we bring love and light into the world. As human beings, we are all connected to each other. To love each other is part of the reason we came into this physical world.

As you read the stories in this section, open your heart, as fully as you can, to receive, to learn and even to be inspired. Take a moment to also reflect. 'Do I have a story of overcoming challenge to share with others?" Or, "Am I currently in the midst of a challenge or am I overwhelmed, and now seeking to grow in faith and trust?"

It would be cathartic and healing for you to tell or write your story and share it with others, wherever you are in your process. Sharing your story releases the hold a past event may have had in defining who you imagined yourself to be. Most importantly, sharing with others offers consolation to them to know that they are not alone in the trials they have faced or currently facing.

When we suffer a challenge, it does not mean that we are bad people or that we are being punished. It means that we have an opportunity to grow and to love ourselves and others more. As human beings, we will each go through a variety of challenging experiences so as to connect, share and love other human beings and life itself.

MY JOURNEY OF FAITH, BREATH, AND SONG

Lisa Stacey Solomon

THE COLLAPSE AND THE CALLING

The day my lungs collapsed, I came face-to-face with both death and divine purpose. I remember the sterile whiteness of the hospital room at Cedars-Sinai in Los Angeles – the sound of machines breathing for me, the silence of my own voice trapped inside. I had already survived a seven-hour surgery that carried only an 18% survival rate. My heart had stopped. Surgeons had sewn me up, but my right lung would not re-inflate. Lying there, I realized this was my coming to Hashem moment – my Jewish form of a "come to Jesus" reckoning. I pleaded, "God, forgive anything I have done to deserve this painful fate. What must I do to re-inflate my lung, to live again?" And then came the answer, clear and deep – "Sing for your people." The voice rose from the depths of my soul. I knew exactly what it meant. For months, I mouthed the words to songs I could not sing, breathing through a machine by night and a tank of oxygen by day. My body was still, but my spirit sang. Even the off-key Filipino singers in my ward became part of my healing – their voices filled the sterile space with color. I had no breath, yet I was learning to live again through sound.

Those four months in the hospital were a wilderness. There was no ability to heal, no certainty I would recover. I spent Passover there, watching the service on closed-circuit TV, a cantor visiting my bedside. My children and ex-husband came daily. Each day was both a test and a blessing. When I finally survived the surgeries – two gastrointestinal procedures, two failed laser operations – I understood: God wanted me to stop. To slow down, to reevaluate my life, my priorities, my dreams. I had been a Marriage and Family Therapist who used creative arts therapies – art, dance, poetry, and music working with addicts, alcoholics, and cancer patients. It was meaningful work but heavy on my soul. I began teaching creative writing and expressive drawing at Miami International Arts College, guiding both seniors and youth. I also taught languages; Spanish, French, and Japanese – in posh private schools. I spoke ten languages. But all my education could not bring back the one thing I had lost: my breath.

THE RETURN TO FAITH

As I healed, I turned to something beyond medicine. I deepened my faith by making Aliyah, moving to Israel, and immersing myself in Hebrew. I spent eight months in Jerusalem, attending weekly cultural programs for Israelis. I visited the graves of rabbis in Tiberias and prayed in the mystical air of Safed, where Chabad energy filled the hills with holiness. I felt renewed – connected not only to God but to the pulse of my people. I vowed to stay aligned with God, to keep my citizenship in Israel, trusting that divine purpose would protect my health. I began visiting Jewish communities across the Diaspora – in the U.S., South America, and Thailand – to write, sing, and share stories of healing and faith. I wanted to shine light, not shame, on our journeys – especially through song.

A NEW CALLING

My Bat Mitzvah had been my first calling – leading prayers weekly, discovering the joy of guiding others in worship. I didn't know it then, but that joy would return to define my adult life. Years later, after my illness, I received another sacred directive. I wrote and performed a one-woman show, "The Singing Rabbi," debuting at the Joshua Tree Fringe Festival in June 2021 and later filmed in Boca Raton. It was a testament to survival, faith, and the power of the voice – a voice that had once gone silent. I even wrote songs with Brazilian Jewish singers who had made Aliyah. Together, we transformed our near-death experiences into music – melodies of resilience and renewal.

FROM BREATH TO BLESSING

I grew personally and spiritually. I led parts of services in Miami, learning to read from the Torah, training in *Davening* (prayer), and joining Jewish choirs in both Miami and Boca. I also sang in interfaith choruses – Jewish, Christian, even opera. Later, I spent a year in Jaffa, Israel, performing as a Jewish piano bar soloist. I sang Persian chants with a ten-piece orchestra. Every note was prayer. Every performance was gratitude. I came to see that art, dance, poetry, and music are all forms of worship. My soul mission for creativity became clear: to merge my background in the arts with my Jewish spiritual life – infusing Shabbat services and communal prayers with artistic expression. This was more than therapy. It was devotion. It was living Judaism through art – consistently, joyfully, authentically.

I've learned to accept life's fragility and its divine purpose. This journey has been my promise to God; to sing for my people. I speak with God now. I know what it means to lead services joyfully – to turn pain into praise, silence into song, breath into blessing.

My voice is no longer just mine. It belongs to the people, to the faith, to the calling that brought me back to life.

Lisa Stacey Solomon is a multidisciplinary artist, educator, creativity coach and writer whose work bridges the worlds of art, spirituality, and healing.

CHOOSING LIFE OVER DEATH: MY BATTLE WITH ANOREXIA

Alana Ruben-Free

Anorexia means loss of appetite. In the 1990s, it carried the highest mortality rate of any mental illness. I was told that up to 25% of anorexics die – not from starvation, but from heart failure. A failure of the heart.

Anorexia disconnected me from myself, my body, my friends, my family, and the world around me. The irony was that the weaker and smaller I became, the safer I felt. Not eating meant not feeling, and not feeling felt safe. Weak and thin, I believed no one could hurt me, nor could I hurt anyone else.

The disease tries to convince you that death is preferable to life, you're simply not needed on the planet. Facts to the contrary have little impact. The unhealthier the body, the unhealthier the mind. Day and night, I examined my psyche seeking out the myriad reasons why neither I nor anyone else could force me to eat. What was I trying to say with my food that I could not say with my words? It turned out a lot.

There were perhaps a hundred or more reasons why I ended up with anorexia in my late twenties, a highly misunderstood disease. How could it be about control and perfectionism, if nothing in my life felt under control, and I could do nothing "perfectly"? Who knew anorexia could be a postpartum condition, triggered by hormonal changes during not only puberty and menopause, but also childbirth?

THE UNRAVELING

Shortly after my son's birth in 1995, while nursing, his pediatrician advised me to eliminate wheat, eggs, garlic, onions, nuts, seeds, beans, tomatoes, soy, and all dairy from my diet. My son's eczema and asthma improved, but my weight plummeted to 100 pounds – the lightest I had been since childhood. When I asked my family doctor about losing twenty pounds, he replied: "Consider yourself lucky – after childbirth, you're lighter, not heavier. Some women get bigger, and you got smaller."

About six months postpartum, strange symptoms emerged: swollen glands, sore throats, breast infections, overwhelming fatigue, bouts of crying, and fears that my heavy, dark mood was contagious. Doctors offered no explanation.

When my son was fourteen months old, my grandmother – who had struggled with depression herself, diagnosed me: "I think you've got depression!" Through her connections in Florida, she found me a psychologist in New York. I felt a glimmer of hope, believing I would soon return to my former self.

On my first visit, the psychotherapist offered a cause: a woman who had always been active, independent, and successful would naturally experience depression staying at home all day. She said that the energy that was meant to go outwards into expression was being turned against myself, leading to depression.

My husband and I had met at business school; he was climbing the Wall Street ladder while I wrestled with diapers, sleep schedules, and other vital tasks that I had to quickly master. I shared with my psychotherapist how dehumanizing my birthing experience had been: I was neglected by the nurses, and my desire for a natural childbirth was dismissed by the doctors, whom I overheard, soon after my son's delivery, making fun of me like schoolboys in a frat house.

After a year working with this therapist, I believed that spending the summer in Israel would cure my chronic lack of appetite. I had always loved the food in Israel; it tasted fresher.

In mid-July, after settling into a vacation rental in Jerusalem with my son, I invited old friends for Friday night dinner. A male friend, who had studied with me in the Negev only a few years before, pulled me aside and asked, "Alana, do you have anorexia?"

Bewildered, I responded, "Why would you think that?" "My sister has it," he replied, "and you look like her."

Over the past year, I had visited various doctors and even a nutritionist, but no one had mentioned the word anorexia.

Close by, I found an energy healer and psychologist who used hands-on healing and magnets. She helped me become more embodied, grounded, and attuned to my inner body's cues. Sometimes I walked home barefoot. As a very bookish, intellectual, I had been ill-prepared for the physical initiation of childbirth and breastfeeding. Mothering took everything that I had physically and emotionally. My therapist in Jerusalem advised me to go back to New York and work with a colleague of hers who integrated Jungian therapy with a range of shamanic disciplines.

Back in New York, I booked an appointment, and then searched the internet for information on anorexia. Reading through the list of symptoms, I realized my friend was right. I checked many of the boxes. I soon began working weekly with a nutritionist specializing in eating disorders. My husband and I continued in marriage counseling, and I read everything I could about the condition. I connected deeply with Marion Woodman's teachings and books.

Once officially diagnosed and in treatment, I assumed recovery would be a piece of cake! The nutritionist prescribed eating more – three meals a day, plus two snacks. Ha! It was the most difficult thing I have ever had to do. I was stunned. I could not make myself eat.

I began with a protein shake with a few Ensure drinks. I felt like an infant, incapable of feeding myself. I could not make myself fill out the food logs, rate my hunger, or track my feelings. The best I could do was write down "not hungry and feel okay." I was humbled. The disease was stronger than my intellect. I had been nominated for a Rhodes Scholarship, and I could not "figure out" how to lift my fork to my mouth. My mind always had a reason why a particular food was inedible.

I believed that God brought me to Torah before bringing me to anorexia so that I would have God on my side as I battled anorexia, which, for me, was the angel of death, Satan, and the *yetzer hara* (evil inclination) all wrapped into one. I read Rabbi Nachman's teaching on the New York subway: "No matter what, one must never despair!" I walked the streets saying to myself, "Every step that I take is to Jerusalem."

"I admitted that I was powerless over my disease…" so on top of weekly therapy, nutritionist appointments, and marriage counseling, I was also attending a lot of 12-Step meetings. Until today, the backbone of my recovery is living "One Day at a Time" and imperfectly turning my life and will over to a Higher Power. Hearing others struggles in the rooms helped me to identify and articulate my deeper issues around eating while giving me a community of women and men who understood my challenges. I identified most with artists and performers. Was this disease a symptom of my rejection of my creative calling?

Since the age of seven, I knew that I was meant to write. What was blocking me?

Just as there was no pill to alleviate the pain of self-abandonment, my psychiatrist confirmed there was no pill to treat anorexia. Whether I would be cured or perish would mostly be dependent upon my willingness to draw to consciousness the beliefs not only blocking my creative flow but also my appetite.

With my therapist, I examined my dreams and unconscious. I became intimate with myself, my dreams, needs, and feelings. Lo and behold, in time, I was able to properly fill out the food logs. I discovered I ate the least the week before my period, and in the feelings column, most days appeared the same word: "anxious." Furthermore, my psychiatrist explained to me that all his artistic clients dealt with anxiety. "Anxiety walks hand in hand with the creative process."

CHOOSE LIFE!

Before my son turned one year old, I began a master's in Jewish Intellectual History. I was committed to fulfilling the Torah commandment to choose life and trusted that if the Torah insisted that life is good, then I must at least, have faith that life is good! I had heard in seminary that "equal to the darkness is the light." I sincerely wanted to experience the light that would be equal to the darkness pinning me down. I was driven by a desire to know how bright life can get.

If I wasn't studying or with my family, I was attending workshops with the leading healers of that time in therapeutic dance, body-mind centering, psychology, and yoga. I began enrolling in writing workshops the year that I decided to end my marriage. Dysfunctional marriage is a diagnostic factor in anorexia. I tried for ten years to conform to a marriage that was relatively "good," but just not good for me.

Once I achieved and maintained my goal weight of 123 pounds, my nutritionist believed I could live free of anorexia. I wanted my life back from this disease. I made a deal with Hashem: I will share my story publicly as a kind of offering, and, in exchange, I wanted Him to free me forever from this illness. In Hebrew, the word for stage, "*bama*," is related to the word "*bima*," the high places where priests made offerings to God.

In 2002, in my first writing class, I met Joy Rose, the founder of the band "Housewives on Prozac" and Mamapalooza. She invited me to be the editor of a journal she had just birthed the year before, named "The Mom Egg." I soon found myself stapling together chapbooks and hanging out with female singer-songwriters at downtown clubs. I started to perform short monologues on stage, and by August 2004, despite being scared to death and trembling, I performed by heart a forty-five-minute one-woman show I wrote, Beginner at Life.

Each performance began with the words: "I want to connect with you. I want you to connect with me. I want connection. The few people who showed up for the first performance at the C-Note were speechless when I was done. My painful vulnerability opened something in them. I would leave each performance feeling naked.

In the spring of 2008, a woman from Australia saw me perform on West 44th Street, and decided to bring the show to Sydney. Thus began the journey of "Beginner at Life." I sat on panels with eating disorder professionals in Canada, Israel, Italy, America, and Australia. I shared about my experiences. I asked members of the audience to write me a note after each show telling me what resonated most for them. I learned how unique is each person's perception, while at the same time how universal, in its depths, the human experience.

On the second run in Sydney, I accompanied the actress and publicist to a juvenile correctional facility for young female offenders. Almost all the women were Aboriginal. While the actress was performing, I wanted the floor to swallow me. The script suddenly sounded like a privileged Upper West Side woman whining about her privileged troubles. I looked at these young women and wondered what stories and traumas they were carrying that landed them in a correctional facility. To my utter surprise, when the performance ended, a young woman said, "I had no idea that a white woman in America has had the same experiences and feelings that we do!" The actress and I spent the whole day with the young women doing a writing workshop. We didn't want to leave. The young "offenders" showered us with love and appreciation. They spoke openly to us, and we experienced connection.

I stipulated, when casting the role of Eden, the main character for Beginner at Life performances, that the actress must be a healthy weight in a mature woman's body. I wanted women to see a woman who was comfortable in her body. Thirty years ago, women in healthy-sized bodies were rarely seen in the media. I wanted to create discussions around the things that had challenged me, like birth, self-love, and eating. After each show, I invited audiences to stay to discuss the show. Sometimes the post-show conversations ran longer than the show.

"Beginner at Life" was performed in Italy in Italian and in Tel Aviv in Hebrew. The translators and the actresses confided in me that working on the play was transformational. One of the translators lost 40 pounds and changed her relationship to her body. One night, a group of heroin addicts in Sydney came to the show and afterwards stood up to say how the show inspired them to think differently about their addiction.

I went on to write two more plays about Eden, but I yearned to turn my plays into participatory art. I wanted my audiences to get the experience of saying the lines, feeling the text in their bodies. I realized this dream in 2015, in Presence=Present, which was featured in the exhibit, "Exalted Mother" at the Jerusalem Biennale. I spent hours in the museum inviting visitors to sit inside a large

500 kilogram, aluminum egg, and speak aloud a text to themselves, God, and/or their loved ones: "I love you. I trust you. I respect you. I appreciate your presence in my life." My hope was that parents would say these words daily to their children from the time that they were born. I wanted every home and heart to be filled with love, respect, trust, and appreciation, the building blocks of my recovery.

Early in the journey, I heard the words in my head: "Evolve or die." Now, I stay on the move and take creative risks that empower me and open creative opportunities for others. I do my best to give other artists, writers, and creatives the feeling of support that I so often need. Participatory art remains central to my purpose, and as a coach, I use everything that I have learned and experienced to help others overcome their personal and creative challenges to reclaim connection, joy, and presence.

When faced with evil, whether within or without, the only place to go is to God. The only force stronger than evil is God. Although I have been free of eating disorders since 2004, I continue to work on healing the root emotional and spiritual issues. Until today, yoga, dance, Torah study, therapy, nutrition, theatre, art, music, writing, 12 Step, poetry, prayers, mask and collage making, dream analysis, and journaling are integral to my life. I am proud to say that I fulfilled my dream of moving to Israel over a decade ago. Undoubtedly, I owe this and many of the other blessings in my life to the years I spent battling anorexia, my greatest teacher.

Alana Ruben-Free is a creativity coach, writer, teacher and theater artist.
www.alanaruben.com

HEALING BEGINS THE MOMENT YOU BELIEVE: A PHYSICAL CHALLENGE LED TO A NEW CAREER

Devorah Gila Berkowitz

I was living on an empty tank, completely out of balance. It was a time when I would collapse from exhaustion after the last child finally drifted off to sleep. Each day I felt like a ping pong ball bouncing back and forth between taking care of my family's needs and everything else on my plate.

One day I somehow found the time to go to the eye doctor. I kept putting it off because I didn't prioritize time to take care of myself. But a friend had said, "It's your eye. We don't mess around with eyes." You see, I had an unusual grey spot in the center of my vision, like a bull's eye that moved every time I looked around. If I looked up, the grey spot went up. If I looked down, the spot went down.

It was a week before Passover, the craziest time in a religious Jewish woman's year. It was a time for shopping, cooking, and cleaning. I was sitting opposite the doctor, with my head poised in that device they use to check your eyes. I remembered this doctor for his sense of humor. He was one to always find something funny to say. But now was no time for jokes. He looked through the lens, first in my right eye, then the left, back and forth, several times. He looked distressed. He told me to wait in the hallway. I watched as he rushed down the hallway, muttering to himself, "Erev Pesach, Erev Pesach!" ("Passover week, Passover week!") I started to become worried. I took out my Tehillim (book of psalms) and started to read. After a while he called me into his office and looked at me with great compassion. In the end, he managed to squeeze out a little sarcasm.

"Mrs. Berkowitz," he said, "where would you like to spend The Passover Seder meal, in Shaarei Tzedek Hospital, or Hadassah

Ein Kerem Hospital?"

"What? Me, in the hospital? With so much to do? The week of Passover?!"

Well, in ten minutes I was sitting in the back of a cab on my way. After two days and many tests, some more painful than others, a neurologist came to see me. He showed me an MRI of my brain. He pointed out several white splotches that hovered on that scan like swatted moths. He called them "UBOs: Unidentifiable Bright Objects, it reminded me of UFOs. I nodded and listened. He spoke on and on...

Then I finally made the connection – the picture of that brain with the white splotches that I was holding in my hands in two dimensions was reflecting what was really going on in my own skull. Those UFOs were flying around inside my head!

Later on I learned that those splotches signified inflammation of the myelin sheath that is supposed to protect the nerves.

So, there it was. Not only was I going blind, I also had brain damage.

When I finally had time alone to reflect on all the events of the previous two days, I sensed a quiet voice rising up from deep within me: You can slow down now. You can stop pushing yourself. You are already doing enough.

Suddenly, I felt calm. I knew I'd be OK. I realized this was my wake-up call.

That very moment was a gateway, a portal to a new reality. I felt a divinely-orchestrated opportunity to make huge changes in my life. And I understood deeply that I had to stop acting like a ping-pong ball ricocheting at every angle, and start taking care of myself so that I could be there for my family in one piece, at peace.

As a result of this surprise wake-up call, including an official diagnosis of an autoimmune disease in the category of Multiple Sclerosis, I hired experts in nutrition, natural healing and energy work. I learned to say "no" and to delegate. I got my husband on my side to help out more in the house.

Most of all, I started appreciating my life and family more, instead of seeing all of my responsibilities as a burden. In the process of taking care of myself, I saw that I was learning powerful life lessons. I knew I had to share these discoveries with other women so they didn't have to burn out like I did, and that was the beginning of my path as a mind-body healing practitioner, gaining experience through my own journey.

My diet overflowed with vegetables and omega 3's. I took supplements and was prescribed salmon three to four times a week. I drank green protein smoothies and went for crania-sacral treatments. Friends offered healing over the phone. I was completely focused on one goal; wellness.

I had bouts of muscle weakness, and suffered from brain fog episodes that lead to depression. Is this what old age is like? I felt decades more than my 40 years.

The colors of my left eye's vision were duller than that of the right side. But week by week I noticed small improvements.

The year went by. I arrived back at the hospital for a follow-up appointment feeling anxious. I wandered through the maze of hallways to the neurology department that I was all too familiar with.

The head doctor of the neurology department, Dr. Miriam, greeted me and smiled warmly. She led me to a room where a practitioner explained the eye exam that I was about to take. I sat down in front of a computer screen and leaned my head uncomfortably into a small frame. Then I waited for flashes of light to appear on the screen. For each one I quickly pressed a button before it disappeared, like a child playing a video game. I played fiercely. I was determined to get every single one right. I had to prove that my eye was better!

But it wasn't a game. It was my health. It was my life.

Afterwards, I wondered, Did I get them all? I felt like I was back in high school, filled with anxiety after a math test. I sat down in one of the hard plastic chairs in the waiting room and read psalms from my small prayer book.

After about twenty minutes, Dr. Miriam showed up and handed me two printouts. She smiled and said, "Your vision is 99% back to normal."

All of a sudden I was overcome by total faith in my ability to overcome this disease. I looked at the doctor in the face with a conviction I had never known before. If God can heal my eye, then surely He can heal the rest of me!

I rushed home, knowing that I was on my way to a complete recovery.

Minutes before dawn, I awoke to the feeling of energy flowing throughout my body, like warm honey. I jumped out of bed in excitement and walked around in amazement. I felt vibrant, energized and alive! No stiffness, no discomfort. I was amazed and in awe.

I will never forget this turning point in my life. It was in that moment eye to eye with Dr. Miriam that I understood deep down that faith can heal us. And with that faith, I have learned how to partner with my Creator to help others like me unlock their innate healing potential.

And to deeply know that not only are we good enough, we are all divine beings just having a very human experience.

Devorah Gila Berkowitz is a medical intuitive, kosher energy healer and mind body practitioner, living in Northern Israel.

CHALLENGE OF ILLNESS LED TO A BOOK AND CAREER AS HEALER.

Tova Reaburn

The life changing incident was learning that my husband had cancer, Malt Lymphoma, in his eyes, which is rare, as it usually located in the stomach. The eye doctor told us there was not much they could do. I was thinking to myself, what an arrogant doctor. He came into the room with a trail of students, never addressing them directly. I have always been of the belief that if a person has a large ego don't believe anything he says. And that is what I told my husband. I didn't know how I was going to drive back home, but God was kind and we hit every stoplight so I was forced to drive slowly.

My brother-in-law, an eye surgeon, suggested Wills Eye in Philadelphia, so we flew to Philadelphia. We spent the month getting my husband radiation treatment. I think leaving Florida to get the treatment in Philadelphia was a good thing. We felt courageous rather than victims. Dr. Shields was remarkable. Why? Because she had a team of students, too. The first year's came in and wrote their notes in pencil, the second years wrote their notes in ink. Dr. Shields questioned each of the doctors and asked for their opinions. The doctor referred us for treatment; radiation every morning for three weeks. At that time, the current treatment had a prognosis of 20% cure. This new doctor had developed a new protocol, which change the outcome to an 80% cure rate. He was scheduled to open a new facility and was leaving after seeing my husband, but decided to come back daily to treat my husband. We stayed at a medical assisted living center.

After treatment, we would go out to the art museum, walk around the city, and visit with other people in the assisted living. We cooked in our room. After the treatment, my husband lost his eyesight in his right eye. He couldn't drive. I knew that the brain makes new connections, and nine months later, he was able to drive, even without regaining his sight.

Cancer changed our entire life. We started in the kitchen, eating only organic, no processed foods, no sugar, nothing white. Exercise became a part of our lives. We rebounded, used the treadmill, weights, and stretched. We use the sauna almost every day. We both kept a grateful journal. When I was terrified before one of his tests, I counted how many times God had helped me during my life. It made me realize that God was still there in our lives.

GOD'S BLESSINGS:

1. God made us leave our home and go to Philadelphia
2. The doctor who invented the new procedure changed the cure rate to 80%.
3. The doctor stayed on to treat my husband.
4. We felt so encouraged, rather than feeling like a victim.

2013

We thought we made it through seven years cancer-free. When we received the news that my husband had a new cancer, Waldenstrom's, we realize that we could not count on the doctors around us. They were into a diagnosis, disease, model, and checking the boxes. Once the doctors name the disease, they no longer look at other possibilities or other treatments. It's never about how to build the body, but to treat a disease. We went on chemotherapy, which caused him to have a toxic reaction on his skin. The chemo had worked and now was on overdrive. His doctor wouldn't take him off the chemo so we went to another doctor. You need to be brave and listen to yourself when you feel something isn't right. He received no treatment and went inter-mission. He lost a lot of his hearing at this time from the radiation. He took up gardening and grew all our vegetables for many years until we moved.

At that time, I came down with Hashimoto's, an autoimmune illness. I started to get into medical research, building the body with nutrients instead of using a medication. It was then that I started working on myself. I was an artist at the time, but I got into the world of colors, not pictures. Every few weeks, God would give me a new area to learn from.

Gratitude, from three colors you can make nine more. Then a new idea would pop into my brain: Healing versus Battling. Battling means there's a winner and a loser; You can't afford to do battle. Another chapter was looking at the pie of your life: where are you not feeling aligned with yourself? Then there were more chapters. These life lessons became a book: *Living in Color.* God's blessings again; I never intended to write a book. I'm not a writer, but I guess I just had too much to say.

Our garden was full of vegetables. It became my husband's focus and new therapy. Between 2013 and 2024, there were hospitalizations and surgeries but not for cancer. In 2024 we moved to be closer to our family, and I got into the Emotion, Body, and Belief Code. After I got certified, I felt so empowered. Everything is energy. I had learned kinesiology many years before, but I never knew how I would get to apply it. Kinesiology is the prerequisite for testing with the codes. Then, when my husband's cancer started to get active again, round three, it was just in time to be able release his negative beliefs around being sick once again. His numbers came down, he was going in the right direction. That was the beginning as we worked on clearing his trapped emotions. Trapped emotions come from not dealing with emotions that come up during stressful times when they get stuck in the body. The Codes enable me to clear these emotions in his organs, glands and systems. From all the holistic lectures available to listen to, I spend about 10 hours of my week learning and have been able to implement many strategies in the healing process God's blessing.

How did I deepen my trust in God? Writing the book, *Living in Color,* helped me to see clearly what I couldn't see before. I go back to the book again and again. I have seen God at work so many times. Sometimes, when I wake up in the morning with an idea that I would not have come up with on my own. I know it's from God.

Right now, I am working on accepting change. I fill my jar with the big stones, love of family and friends, then the pebbles, things I like to do, or things I have learned to want to do because they support me. Then the sand, which are things that will not be important in a few days, a week. Challenge creates opportunities that are beyond what we imagine are possible.

Tova Reaburn, Author of *Living in Color,* and healer

LEAVING A BAD MARRIAGE

Anonymous

From an abusive marriage to service and joyful life.

I didn't know at age 18 what a narcissist was. My ex-husband fits every description. Every movement, control, manipulation, lies, hurtful and showing everyone else what a different person he was. Everyone thought he was so wonderful.

I was twenty and a Junior at NYU, when we married. He was charming, a poet, and the sweetest. My wise mother, the first time she met him, told me to run, that I would cry my whole life from him and his children. That his genes were strong and he would turn them against me. And during my divorce, he did. His sweetness was the bait. It was my generation to stay in a marriage, and keep my family whole. I should have known when he pushed my thirteen year old brother down icy steps because he didn't shovel at the exact time he was told.

Life was a fairytale, and a nightmare at the same time. I grew up in a home of love. He grew up in a home of dysfunction. From early on, I was verbally and emotionally abused. I never could nourish his happiness level. I was able to brush it off because I became a young mother, and lived in a glass home. Everyone saw a beautiful life, but no one knew the inside.

He loved his drugs; marijuana all day, and 21 years of cocaine. He physically abused our eldest daughter three times. She was angry with me for years as I stayed in the marriage. I feared what life would be like for my children if I left.

His bankruptcy, due to cocaine use, moved us to Jacksonville. That is where the abuse increased. When I was six months pregnant with our son, I was physically abused. He pushed me against the kitchen counter, and choked me. I grabbed my youngest daughter and went to the home of my Rabbi. This rabbi instructed me to return to my marriage.

The second time, I was nursing our son, and he pushed me down on a ceramic floor, choking me. And, once again, we fled to my Rabbi. He once again instructed me to return to the marriage as my ex requested.

One time, when I was hosting 25 guests for Rosh Hashanah dinner, my husband did not even sit at the table. He did not speak to me for nine months. At first it was so difficult, and then I loved his silence.

Our son was seven when I finally decided to leave the marriage, and move back North, near to my family. Everything was in place. My ex had a psychiatrist in NYC, who encouraged me to go on vacation and separate as friends. I didn't want to, and ended up going on a cruise, sleeping in separate beds. On day three, as he was high on cocaine, he suffered a heart attack at the espresso bar. It was a spasm, and we flew home on a private jet with a doctor and nurse. That was his strongest manipulation. "How can I leave a sick man, the father of my children, I stayed."

When our son was fourteen, on a tennis court, my ex asked if I would have an open marriage. I knew there were two women on the side, and perhaps a man. And so, the next day when he left on a business trip with one of the women, I went to an attorney.

A power of strength infused me. The divorce was brutal; all lies, and then came the third physical abuse in front of my mother and son. My mother called 911 and he was arrested as he was choking me, throwing me against a bannister. Perhaps the abuse was a blessing, as I was able to raise money to help build a larger shelter for abused women and their children because of it.

My life changed. I left Ponte Vedra and moved to South Florida. There I became part of *Shalom Bayit,* an organization for abused Jewish women. I soon had to stop and get my own strength. I worked three jobs including cleaning homes as my electricity was shut off. I sold cars, missing my son's Lacrosse games, grew my own business, a travel company, that I continue to operate until today.

This period of time was so difficult. A man who hurts the mother of his children, also hurts his children. He travelled with friends, with the women, sent gifts, while I suffered. I sold my jewelry to send my son to prom. The abused daughter took his manipulative side, not talking to me for one and a half years. Ten years ago, our son went to Iceland with his father, returning, and didn't talk with me for a year and a half. My tears could not stop. I was with my mother crying telling her how I am filled with pain. The child I did everything I could for. She was so wise, and said God is not blind, and your tears will be the pain your ex will receive.

He now suffers ten years with ALS, where he cannot control his own body. He refuses to give me my Jewish divorce, a get. He still has an insurance policy in my name, that he refuses to give. I never will talk with him again. Has he learned the lessons of life? It would appear that his pain has not allowed him to remove his narcissistic soul. Can you imagine the day our son was married, he went to the hospital having an attack, calling his children right before the ceremony.

In the divorce, I lost everything. The judge was a good old boy, and let him get away with everything. But, God did not.

Later on in years, **I decided to volunteer in the Lotus House in Miami, a unique environment for battered women and their children. I wanted to help with the children, and the babies, while the mothers rehabilitated. It is the most incredible environment you can imagine.**

Then, Covid came, and no one was allowed in.

My story actually is beautiful. I waited for the right man to come to my life. I continued with a strong faith, believing if I can help other women, even in the workforce, Hashem would be compassionate. Soon, I fell in love with a kind, supportive, loving man, where our lives together are one in harmony. We laugh, and even dance in the kitchen.

By Anonymous

LOVE IS STRONGER THAN FEAR

Jodi Samuels

I had a mother's intuition that something was wrong with my pregnancy six weeks before Caila was born. Even now, I can still feel that visceral jolt when I think back to that exact moment. My husband, a medical doctor, along with all the other professionals, reassured me that everything was fine. All the tests looked perfect. But the feeling lingered, deep, unshakable, and hauntingly real.

Although I was never one to truly pray, I remember how desperately I prayed that day in the operating room as I was being prepped for my cesarean. I pleaded with the Almighty to give me strength for whatever lay ahead. Even as I write these words, I find myself holding my breath. Breathe, I remind myself. Just breathe.

Looking back, I believe God was preparing me. I have come to understand the saying: You never know how strong you are until being strong is your only choice.

When the doctor asked if I had done genetic testing and then gently told me he suspected my beautiful newborn had Down syndrome, a storm of emotion overtook me. I thought of my older cousin with Down syndrome, born in the 1970s and institutionalized at birth, an experience that brought deep family trauma. I thought of another cousin with a disability and felt crushed by the weight of what I now had to share with my family.

Then came the fear. What would this mean for my life? For my marriage? For my other children? I was the hostess extraordinaire, our home was a revolving door of thousands of guests every year. I was an ambitious woman, on my way to visiting my 40th country, driven by dreams of gracing the pages of Forbes or Fortune. Suddenly, my identity, my plans, my sense of self, all seemed to hang in the balance.

But in the midst of fear, I did what I knew best: I took action. I reframed the situation. I chose to believe that no matter what Caila's challenges would be, I would help her achieve 110 percent of her potential. If I didn't like what I saw in the world, I would work to change it.

That commitment became my calling. I found my voice. I became a leader and an advocate for disability inclusion. I realized that I could influence how a community responds to difference and that one family's courage could transform how others see the world.

Eighteen years later, this journey has been both hard and deeply rewarding. I am grateful beyond words that my husband has shared every step of this path with me. Together, we have poured our hearts into changing Caila's reality and we hope, the future for all children with disabilities.

Over these years, I have experienced a paradox of emotions: pride and joy intertwined with fear and uncertainty. Caila is a remarkable young woman, vibrant, empathetic, determined, and full of light. She is a beautiful soul inside and out. I often vacillate between immense pride in her accomplishments and a lingering fear of the unknown. I constantly question whether I've made the right choices, whether I've done enough, whether I've pushed too much, or not enough.

When Caila finished fourth grade, I told her how proud I was of her achievements and how special she is. She smiled and replied, "I'm special, and also special needs." That moment grounded me. It reminded me of our family mantra, inspired by Professor Reuven Feuerstein: If you love me, don't accept me as I am. True love means believing in potential and always challenging growth, while never being disappointed if the goal isn't reached.

I often tell Caila, I will change the world for you, but I would not change you for the world.

Yet as I write this letter to myself, I realize one of the goals I now need to challenge is my own role in her life. I have invested thousands of hours in therapy, advocacy, and support. But I also know that a parent's job is to raise a soul, to prepare her to live fully and independently, with purpose and dignity.

Now it's time for me to show her that I believe in her by stepping aside, by allowing her to forge her own way, to dream her own dreams, to shape her own world.

I love Caila deeply. My dreams for her are vast, but ultimately, I know this truth; Her life is her own. Her journey is sacred.

And her light, her very being, is the greatest blessing of all.

Jodi Samuels is a global speaker, author, entrepreneur, community builder, and founder of Jewish International Connection and Jody's Voice podcast.

THE OTHER SIDE OF DARKNESS LED TO A CAREER AS YOGA TEACHER AND HEALER

Rachel Yona Shalev

After twelve long years, I finally finish my memoir – a lifetime of struggle and survival pressed into pages, a thin thread of faith running through it all. I've clung to Viktor Frankl's wisdom; that there is meaning in suffering, and that it is always worth living for. When I close the manuscript, a rush of accomplishment washes over me – immediately followed by a deep, aching sadness.

My life has been so very hard. And it was always supposed to end up great.

But what if it hasn't? Lately, it's been too much – too many losses, too many roles stripped away. The world no longer feels safe, especially since October 7. Not even two years later, here in Israel, the devastation still hums in my bones. It feels impossible to relax. Then, a few days after the Iranian war, my nervous system collapses. My back twinges. My left side seizes. The pain builds until I'm jumping out of my skin. Why has this descended on me? What could I have possibly done to deserve it?

Hours later, I'm in the Emergency Room, writhing on the floor, a CT scan whirring above me, morphine sliding into my veins. Body and soul, I feel shattered. "I can't do this anymore. I want to give up," I whisper to my younger sister -- the one who has only ever known me as unbreakable. She rests a hand on my back. "You don't know what you're saying. You'll get through this. You always do." It's true. I always do. But at what cost?

I trace my way back through the so-called choices I never truly had. I didn't choose my childhood, though it set the stage for all that followed. My parents were good people, but like many of their generation in the 1960s, they didn't know how to parent. While there were no drugs or alcohol, but there was abuse and neglect. Later came the abusive marriage I escaped from penniless, carrying two small children. Years of single parenting were shadowed by fear and depletion, trying to raise a child with emotional disabilities.

I still feel the day I left him with his unstable father nine years old, a pain and guilt that may never leave me. For years I lived in a fog, picturing my beautiful boy suffocating under a darkness I couldn't lift. I wanted to fling off the darkness and reveal his light, to breathe my love into him, to let him to know he was safe. Instead I lay awake knowing he might be going to bed hungry, alone, and afraid. Knowing I was powerless to help him.

All of it is etched written into my body. No wonder it's been breaking down for years.

Another sleepless night, painkillers, sleeping pills. I can't fight anymore. Not without the body that has always been my greatest ally. I'm a yoga teacher. A healer. How can this be happening? I always believed things would get better. Could it be that it won't? Could this be as good as it gets, or worse?

I think back to the chapter that felt like redemption. After years of loss, I was reunited with my second soul mate – my one true love. He held me, cared for me, gave me the safety I had never known. Sixteen years of love felt like a reward for surviving.

And then, without warning, he left me for another woman. The shock dropped me back into survival, into inconsolable grief. Now, after the war, my one attempt at love in my 60s has failed. I face the possibility of growing old alone – a loveless life.

I picture my future; a caregiver wheeling me through the park, chocolate milkshake in my shaking hand. Or worse, slumped in a dim room, waiting out the hours.

I keep forgetting the deep spiritual truth: After every descent, there's an Aliyah – an ascent toward the promised land. Maybe we're wired to forget, so when the rise comes, it startles us with its light.

Over time, I have come to celebrate that I am a writer. A healer, a therapist, a yoga teacher. I've learned to sit alone with my breath, my pain, my losses. The years have changed me.

Grief has cracked my heart open, leaving more space for others, and between the cracks, space for me to breathe.

The pain remains, but it has transformed into wisdom, into radical compassion for myself and others. It has trained me to hold everything I feel, and still offer light. A *bodhisattva*.

Some days, I want to stay wrapped in grief, holding my untouched, aging body in tenderness, avoiding the world. But when I allow myself to sink into the deepest valleys, something unexpected appears. Magic.

It always takes me by surprise, because it's never remembered, only found.

I remember that this moment is my life and it is my choice to decide want to do with it, right here, right now. How do I want to feel? How do I want to make others feel? I remember to make each moment count, like our holy matriarch Sarah, whose every moment counted.

I pull myself up.

I answer the messages. I show up to teach.

I invite friends to dance

I give my time and energy to healing others.

Even in darkness, I say yes.

I make the dreaded doctor's appointment. I do the paperwork.

I clear the clutter.

And somehow, joy returns.

I feel it in the cool Jerusalem air after a heatwave. In the taste of a fresh fig.

In water running over my hands as I wash dishes.

In the bliss of gazing into a newborn's eyes. In sitting beside a friend in the hospital.

In preparing food for the sick.

When my back aches, when I see the suffering in my son's eyes, when loneliness closes in, when I bear witness to the darkness of our world, I remind myself:

Stay here.

Proceed with joy. This moment is a gift. I can do this.

Stay with the inhale. Stay with the exhale. My breath has never failed me.

This moment is good. It is enough.

Rachel Yona Shalev, yoga teacher, author and healer

CHAPTER 4

LIFE IN ISRAEL ON OCTOBER 7TH AND BEYOND

Life in Israel has always had its challenges. Since the modern establishment of this Jewish state, Israel has faced almost continuous efforts by its much larger neighbor nations to destroy it. All these wars failed to diminish Israel in size and power. Because of these wars, Israel actually regained all of Jerusalem, Gaza, Judea Samaria, Golan Heights, enabling Israel to reclaim lands that were all part of the original kingdom of Israel thousands of years ago. Efforts to engage in random and frequent acts of terrorism against civilian populations also failed to weaken the resolve of people to live in Israel.

Nevertheless, October 7th and its aftermath ushered in the most challenging times for Jews in Israel since the holocaust. On October 7th itself, over a thousand people were murdered and hundreds taken hostage, from babies to elderly. Among those murdered and held hostage in Gaza tunnels were accounts of such cruelty that was not even seen during times of Nazism. On

October 7th, babies were beheaded and burned in front of parents, women were raped in front of family members. The evil displayed by Hamas was beyond anything previously imaginable. Unlike the Nazis who chose to hide most of their atrocities as best as they could, many Hamas terrorists were so proud of their exploits, they even filmed them to publicly share them and make their relatives proud.

As of late 2025, the Israeli Defense Ministry reported that a total of 1,152 Israeli soldiers including IDF, Israeli police and Shin Bet, have died since the war began on October 7, 2023. An alternative report from Israeli officials specified that at least 913 of these were Israel Defense Forces (IDF) soldiers. Because Israel is such a small number of people, this is a significant amount of soldiers to be killed.

After October 7th, the intensity of challenges increased for all people living in Israel. The civilian population of Israel has had to endure frequent calls to bomb shelters due to rockets from Iran, the Houthis from Yemen, Hamas in Gaza and Hezbollah in Lebanon. Many Israeli soldiers have been wounded and murdered. Thousands of people have had to relocate and seek shelter in different communities. Everyone in Israel has been touched by October 7th. Almost everyone in Israel rose to be of greater service than ever before in small and dramatic ways. Just remaining in Israel at this time of challenge was an act of service. Many Israelis living out of Israel at this time chose to return there as soon as possible.

In spite of all these challenges or because of them, this time period after October 7th has initiated a heightened rise in faith and prayer within Israel. More secular people are now seeking connection with God, with Torah learning and even beginning to become Torah observant. Though the divisions between various people in Israel remain, there is greater unity because everyone recognizes that the enemies of Israel do not distinguish between those on the right or left politically.

A spiritual and economic renaissance is now emerging in Israel from these challenges. Even though many in the world may still seek to denigrate Israel with false accusations of genocide, famine and oppression, the light and love of Israel is shining brightly for those who have eyes to see and a heart to feel what is truly present.

In spite of all these wars, Israel continues to lead and share its advanced technological discoveries, uplifting the quality of life, economies and the defense of nations around the world. These wars have taken a toll on Israelis but they have also deepened their love and connection with each other and to fulfilling the soul mission of the Jewish people as prescribed to them in the Bible.

ACCOUNTS OF PEOPLE LIVING IN ISRAEL ON OCTOBER 7TH

VOICES AT THE EDGE OF REDEMPTION

Shira Lankin Shleps

"I can still feel that first moment. That very first siren still lives in my bones. It was like living in slow motion; my daughter woke me on that Simchat Torah morning, and I was sick in bed. I had been fighting an infection and was curled up, in pain. The way the siren reverberated off the Jerusalem mountains surrounding our home, echoing through the valley, building to a crescendo as it reached our neighborhood – bleeding into my already fevered body – I'll never forget it as long as I live.

I recall the way my heart woke up, how my muscles came alive as I struggled to get out of bed and hobble to the bomb shelter. Adrenaline began to pump through me as I ran – adrenaline that would become my constant companion over the next two years, as I was called to experience life-saving acts or witness, on our screens and in our reality, horrors I never could have dreamed of in my worst nightmares.

But in that first moment, I knew. I had a realization, with fierce certainty, that everything was about to change. In my mind, I heard, "This is it. It's finally here. It's finally come." In the first few weeks of the war, I coined it "the ultimate battle between good and evil." The evidence was so stark, so black-and-white, so horrifying, that there was nothing to do but witness it all and do our best to keep our sanity in check and our families going.

My brothers were called to war that day, and my calling during those months and years was to support my sisters – their pregnancies, and their children – while their fathers were away protecting our borders. A close friend declared during that time that we were living in "cities of women": women supporting women through impossible moments and sleepless nights.

Together, my extended family slept on mattresses in the living room because our bedrooms were too far from the shelter to reach in time. While everyone slept around us, my husband and I would whisper in the night about whether the gates around our home would be enough to protect us should our neighborhood be infiltrated, as surrounding neighborhoods had already been. We had no weapons at home, and we made plans for nightmare scenarios alongside our neighbors, never knowing what the next days would bring.

We sat all day in a fog, our newsfeeds full of missing or murdered people. Work stopped. Life stopped. With every scroll, there were new faces – never the same one twice; there were so many. I remember being dissociated from horror, sitting there holding my children and my niece, running when called to, numbing in the silence. I lay awake all night grappling with the possibility that maybe I had been wrong about where we were on the messianic timeline; I had believed we were close to redemption, past the most painful parts of our Jewish history, on the way to peace and blessing. The death all around us shocked me to my core. The hostages, we thought, we would never see again.

In those endless hours, I thought about God and His plan – begging for some sort of sign, some semblance of an answer, a glimmer of hope. They came in stories from the battlefield: an enemy gun that jammed and couldn't discharge, a rocket aimed at a major city that blew into the sea. They came in acts of service all around me, in the way people cared for their families and neighbors. My house filled with donations from the diaspora: weapons and protective gear, socks and hand warmers, gun holsters and headlamps, drones smuggled into the country. My husband spent his days distributing gear to units stationed across Israel and in Gaza. Those stories poured in too: the headlamp that saved a unit because the soldier leading the charge could see at night, the drones that found terrorists, the protective vest plates that empowered young men to go out and fight for our people.

My brother called me from the *shetach*; the field – where his unit was stationed, protecting kibbutzim on the Syrian border. He told me how it felt like time was blending, generations and cycles of war and survival morphing into one Jewish experience. As third-generation Holocaust survivors, it was surreal, and we tried to see our lives through our grandparents' eyes, through our children's eyes. Mostly, we just tried to keep our eyes open and survive each day, trying to keep our stamina going.

Months passed, and we lived in a country in uproar – in pain, in protest, in service. We helped wherever we could, supporting our greater family, our children, our people. Every day, we woke up to a cloud of suffering, of heaviness, of grief and fear that permeated the land. You could see everyone around us ebbing and flowing with the rollercoaster of the news; death announcements, successes, near-misses. I spent much of my days giving and receiving support from my female friends, offering each other strength to get through another day. Another crisis. Another moment of uncertainty.

I told them I didn't believe we were here only to suffer. I said that our souls had chosen to enter this world at this exact moment so we could witness it. We were meant to be present for our people, to know the breaking firsthand, so that when the time for healing came, we would understand what was needed. Only through experience could we truly do that work. Every day, I reminded them that this time period of war would not last forever. One day, we would move into a new season of blessing. And when that time arrived, we would be called to look clearly at what we had been through and become part of the solution – to help move us forward, toward a redeemed future.

I never stopped believing that day would come. I carried a deep sense of knowing that there was work waiting for me, and I had yet to be called. I thanked God every day that I was living in Israel, that I could firsthand bear witness to our incredible nation. Presence became an essential part of my life. But I still carried fear. We were terrified of Iran and Hezbollah; the country was a mess. People were living day to day without enough resources, many evacuated from their homes, border communities terrorized in the North and South, rockets falling across the country, new names of soldiers killed every day, hostages coming home in pockets of relief, but most still suffering, their families crying out in agony. The fever pitch of the war mounted.

The first Pesach came, and the nights before Seder, we were attacked by Iran for the first time. The night was absolutely surreal; a sci-fi, spiritualist fever dream. We watched missiles and drones heading toward us on our screens and waited for hours as doom slowly approached. In the hours before they arrived, I received messages from friends and loved ones, reaching out not to say goodbye, exactly, but to say "I love you." We didn't know if we would ever speak again, so we left nothing unsaid.

At 2 a.m. they broke our airspace, and we ran to the shelter alongside our neighbors, our hearts in our throats, having no clue if we would survive the night or what world we would walk out to when it was over. It was the largest missile attack in world history at that point, and while we were in the shelter, we learned that the majority of the rockets had been shot out of the sky by our army and our allies. It was hard to believe; it felt like a miracle on par with the splitting of the sea, the stopping of the sun in the sky.

I walked out of the bomb shelter that night a changed person. We had experienced the most revealed miracle of our lifetime, and by Seder night, when we began to sing the steps of the Seder, the tears would not stop flowing. All night, we talked about the way God intervened for the Jews, from the redemption of Egypt to our salvation that very week. We finally saw ourselves in the context of Jewish history. The messianic timelines came back into focus, and we were in dialogue with the Divine.

The whole week of Pesach, I processed. And on the seventh day, the day when the Jewish people finally crossed the Red Sea to freedom – I had what I call a "Divine Download." An idea arrived in my mind in its entirety, as if it were not my own. A calling, finally. It didn't feel like my idea, but something I was charged with creating and bringing into the world.

It began with thinking about Miriam the Prophetess, and how she and the women of the Exodus generation (according to the midrash) knew redemption was on its way and had their musical instruments ready on their backs – prepared to sing when geulah came.

Our sages teach that the generation of Egypt was redeemed in the merit of the *Nashim Tzidkaniot,* the righteous women. And we know that the final redemption will mirror the redemption from Egypt. So the question emerged: if the women of Egypt prepared themselves for geulah, what can we, the women of our own generation, do to hasten the final redemption?

I decided that we needed to prepare to sing like Miriam; to take the trauma of the war, the revelation of God through His revealed miracles, and open our mouths to give voice to this time. Thus, the idea for *Az Nashir,* We Will Sing Again: Women's Prayers for Our Time of Need was born. It became an anthology of prayers written by Jewish women in Israel, addressing the unique experiences and urgent issues of living in Israel in a post-October 7th world. Written by female Torah scholars, teachers, spiritual leaders, activists, poets, writers, and masters of artistic expression, these prayers gave voice to the myriad complex emotions, needs, and hopes that arose in that time.

This siddur- companion followed in the footsteps of our ancestors, emulating a long tradition of Jewish women writing their own tefillot, techinot, and piyutim – an organic outpouring of our hearts, in our own mother tongues. From prayers that engaged directly with the new challenges that emerged after the war began, to prayers exploring the interconnectedness of national tragedy and mundane, intimate moments, we touched the fullness of our lived experience.

We included prayers for the release of the hostages, sending a child off to war, gratitude for a spouse returning safely, surviving a rocket attack, parenting in crisis, loss of a loved one, wrestling with infertility, illness, pregnancy, dating, motherhood, and more – with national tragedy acknowledged alongside personal struggle. We included women's mitzvoth – candle-lighting, challah, mikveh; at that challenging time. The complexities and blessings of Shabbat during wartime. Mental and physical well-being under prolonged grief and pressure.

Grappling with emotions such as anger, grief, hope, impatience. Personal growth in suffering and in miracles. Expressions of *emunah* (faith) and *bitachon* (trust). Reaffirmation of Jewish identity in the face of antisemitism.

And there it was; the reason I was here, living through this moment. We created a movement, and alongside my contributors and editors, we traveled across Israel and hosted events: nights of song, sorrow, and faith, of healing and hope. We read prayers aloud to God and held space for the unique moment in history we were living through. We came together as a community, holding each other through these footsteps that precede the messianic era, expressing to one another, and to the Divine, the deepest truths of our souls. Dreaming about the world we would rebuild together.

And so we gathered, night after night; women of every age and story, breath and heartbeat. We whispered ancient words and offered new ones, braided grief with hope, let our throats vibrate with prayer. We stood exactly where Miriam once stood: trembling at the edge of trauma, witnessing God in action, trying to make sense of it all through gratitude.

I hope that, in many generations from now, scholars will look back on this body of work and see it as a time capsule. They will be able to pick up and hold our faith in their hands, and see how the women of faith processed this ultimate battle of good and evil, how we loved each other and our people, how we stood fast in our land. How we sacrificed and prayed. How we believed in our joint destiny and how we dreamed of a new reality of peace that would last forevermore.

I learned that healing begins not with answers, but with voice. That redemption unfolds not all at once, but in the quiet choices we make to show up for each other.

We are still walking through the sea. The waters are high, the future opaque. We are following a bright pillar of fire that is leading us through this time. Each prayer is a step forward, each song a torch held through the night.

And when the dawn breaks – as it has already begun – we will already be singing.

Shira Lankin Shleps, MSW. Writer, editor, workshop facilitator, Founder of the Leaders project magazine. www.shvillicenter.org

HAIFA'S WAITING PLACE

Liane Grunberg Wakabayashi

It looks like I can throw away my alarm clock. Hezbollah has it timed now, waking Haifa around 7 a.m. with missiles that trigger the air raid sirens and send me running in my pajamas to the *miklat,* our apartment building's shelter. Afterwards, I go home – a ten-second walk – and fetch thick gloves for garden work. Raking leaves and fallen bougainvillea calms me down. But how much raking can one do?

Two years into my life in Haifa, Iran is threatening to flatten the glorious Carmel mountain range with what it calls a "crushing response." This intense war, *Operation Swords of Iron,* is a profound test of wills. Theodor Seuss Geisel, the late, great Dr. Seuss, put it all into perspective in his final children's book, *Oh, the Places You'll Go*. The story follows a character traveling through time and space only to arrive at "the waiting place," where everyone is just waiting for something to happen.

Well, here we are. All of Israel is in the waiting place. We're waiting in Haifa. Tel Aviv is waiting. Jerusalem is waiting. Even the Arab villages in the north, which ironically receive a disproportionate share of missile fire – are waiting. In this small country, nowhere is an island.

"You're off to Great Places! You're off and away! You have brains in your head. You have feet in your shoes. You can steer yourself any direction you choose."

That's easy for Dr. Seuss to say. In our daily lives here, many of us feel we can't steer ourselves anywhere. It leads me to wonder: is this the whole point of being an Israeli? To commit to being here, in whatever part of the country we call home, no matter what?

In this uncertainty, I'm discovering opportunities in Haifa that were inconceivable before October 7th, 2023. I find myself wanting to be more useful than I ever imagined possible. My feet are taking me toward volunteering, and I'm learning that the word "volunteering" is misleading; it's not a one-way favor. The more I do, the more I connect to a solid purpose for loving my life in Israel.

I saw a message on the "Ahuza Anglo Community" WhatsApp group; a large number of wounded soldiers were being released from the hospital, and volunteers were needed to bring cheer to those remaining. I signed up. Ahuza is an upscale Haifa neighborhood with wide balconies and sunset views of the Mediterranean, and for some reason, I assumed the hospital would be on that side of Mount Carmel.

When I received the directions, I discovered the hospital, Bnei Zion, was so close to my home in the Hadar neighborhood that I only had to climb two mountain staircases to get there.

On the appointed day, I entered a reception area overflowing with colorful donuts and homemade cakes. Tables were piled high with t-shirts and sneakers, generously donated by a major brand. The atmosphere was festive, like a carnival. The recovering young men were in high spirits, enjoying the treats and visits from family and friends. There wasn't anything for us volunteers to do. Our role, it turned out, was simply to bear witness. In that moment, it crystallized for me: it was enough to be a fly on the wall, to see how things are done in Israel. On the day these severely wounded soldiers were leaving the hospital after the most life-threatening event of their young lives, they were sent home with a wonderful party.

As much as I want to volunteer, it's not always simple. You often need a car. Thankfully, my new friends Lia Shinozaki Kagan and her husband Henri, immigrants from Brazil, were volunteering almost daily to help farmers pick their crops. They kindly picked me up before 7 a.m. so we could reach a cucumber greenhouse in the cooler part of the morning. We worked mostly in a calm, meditative silence.

It was only months later, when Lia stopped by my house, that I learned why she embraces life here with such vigor. That's all I knew about her; that she was a first-generation Japanese-Brazilian with relatives in Japan. Then, as we were carrying parts of a sukkah to her car, an air raid siren chose its moment to blast overhead. We dashed into my building's *miklat*. There, during the long minutes of waiting, Lia told me her story: she had miraculously survived the deadly 1995 Kobe Earthquake, pulled from the rubble five hours after her dormitory collapsed on top of her.

As I took in her story, I related it to my own thirty years in Japan. We looked at each other, and the same thought occurred to us; somehow, we feel safer here in Israel, no matter what. With God running the show, what is there to fear?

Our farmer was generous and sent us home with more cucumbers than we could eat. I thought about knocking on the doors of neighbors I didn't know to share the bounty. I hesitated, though, because my neighbors don't exactly meet my standard of tidiness. But a free online Zoom session by Haifa psychiatrist Dr. Naftaly helped me put my petty gripes aside. A few days after I traded cucumbers for smiles, the piles of junk, gravel, and a rusty toaster oven in our shared space magically disappeared.

Another WhatsApp post led me to the home of a family sitting *Shiva* for their son, Amit Hayut, a 29-year-old soldier. The thought of attending was intense; he had been killed in Lebanon just the day before. I didn't know the family. I wasn't a friend or a neighbor. It's only in Israel, I think, that I would dare do such a thing.

How do you introduce yourself when you step into an apartment filled with people who knew and loved him? I explained that I was a writer for The Jerusalem Post. My work as a journalist has often pushed me far out of my comfort zone and into situations mirroring the tragedies unfolding daily in Israel. In a gazebo-like tent outside, soldiers from Amit's battalion gathered to talk about their commander, calling him "the best of all best friends."

Visiting the family, hearing soldiers recall their friend's last moments, and seeing plates of mouth-watering food go largely uneaten, the ritual of *Shiva* brings the enormity of the loss into sharp relief. I eventually found Tsippi, the fallen soldier's mother, holding a picture of her beloved son, who was now headline news for the worst of reasons. Amit Hayut was 29, far too young to go.

"Out there things can happen. And frequently do to people as brainy as you."

Haifa is a brainy town. We have the Technion, the University of Haifa, and Matam; our own Silicon Valley overlooking the Mediterranean. We have army, naval, and air force bases that send fighter jets across the sky multiple times a day. We have Rambam Hospital, with its 2,000-bed fortified underground facility ready for triage in a pinch – God forbid.

But much about Haifa isn't smart at all, making life in wartime miserable, if not dangerous. The very thing that makes Haifa picturesque – Mount Carmel rising like a crown over the city, is also its most dangerous feature. Neighborhoods are built on its slopes, connected by highways that run through nature reserves called wadis. These open slopes offer clear views of the sea and the port, but they also leave us vulnerable to missile fire from Lebanon and Iran. My phone's GPS often tells me I'm in Lebanon; my clock app says I'm on Amman time.

Heading home from Haifa's largest mall, I was walking along a boulevard flanked by one of these wadis when it occurred to me; if a siren went off right now, I would have nowhere to run. Sidewalks were deemed essential here, but bomb shelters were not. What was I supposed to do, stay home in fear? In that moment, I don't think I've ever been happier to see a city bus pull up to the curb to carry me to safety.

"And then things start to happen. Don't worry. Don't stew.Just go right along. You'll start happening too."

I moved to Haifa because it's a great place to be an artist and a writer. Climbing the steep mountainside staircases helps me sit down and write. Meandering walks under tall Cypress trees inspire my paintings. I even keep a separate album on my phone for photos of soldiers and demonstrators. The soldiers, men and women keeping us safe at such young ages, are like rock stars to me. The demonstrators are often older folks maintaining a vigil for the hostages at a public square, which has become part art installation, part shrine, with posters of the hostages attached to empty yellow chairs.

The dedication of these people seeped into my imagination and shifted my outlook from that of an observer to a participant. Between picking cucumbers and painting scenes of daily life, there's no time to worry, no time to stew.

And yet, I'd be lying if I said my heart doesn't race when I hear that evil-sounding siren, a sound that saves our lives even as it threatens to pull us into despair. We've been dealing with these sirens almost daily for a month, and it never gets easier. Still, I know there's nowhere I'd rather be.

As the great Dr. Seuss – a lifelong Lutheran whose *neshama* (soul) came into this world through Jewish-German parents – so aptly put it, we have what it takes to be resilient. A journey through a bizarre land, seeing things we never imagined, doesn't mean we have to run.

"You have brains in your head. You have feet in your shoes.You can steer yourself any direction you choose."

The weather is balmy, and the leaves are turning golden. Facing this latest hurdle in Israel's complex history, standing together with the resilient people of Haifa simply feels like the right thing to do.

Liane Wakabayashi, author of memoir *The Wagamama Bride*
www.genesiscards.com

LOSS OF A SOLDIER SON IN GAZA WAR LED TO ESTABLISHING HEALING CENTER IN TZFAT FOR SOLDIERS.

Jen Airley

On the 5th of Kislev, 21-year-old Binyamin Airley hy"d fell in Gaza. Since then, Binyamin's mother Jen has been an inspiration to all of Am Yisrael, speaking openly from the heart with extraordinary strength and faith. Rabbi Aron White spoke with Jen to hear about Binyamin's life and legacy.

"Binyamin wanted to join an elite army unit. He passed the test for paratroopers, and joined Unit 101. He was drafted in August 2021 and really loved the yeshiva boys he was with.

He was taken up to *shamayim* (heaven) on November 18th. He was actually supposed to be finishing his service in December 2023, but he probably would have stayed on longer. He wouldn't have been able to return to yeshiva while the war was still going on – he wanted to continue fighting and couldn't stand the idea that others would be fighting while he would be far from the war.

We were in Ramat Beit Shemesh for Yom Tov. Once we saw all the surreal scenes of all the soldiers driving on streets that are usually silent on Shabbat, I knew that Binyamin had also been called up. That night, he called to say that he was at a base in the north, and from there they were helicoptering down south.

His unit went to Nir Am, a kibbutz adjacent to Sderot, checking house by house to make sure there were no terrorists. After a few days, he called from some landline to tell us he was okay. After some time, his unit went to a paratrooper training base for intensive training to prepare for going into Gaza. Before they went in, the army hosted a family picnic on October 27th just outside the base. We had a couple of hours all together. On Monday they gave in their phones and on Tuesday they went into Gaza, where he fought for two and a half weeks before he was killed.

He trained as a "Negevist," a role given to the stronger soldiers who operate the Negev machine gun. When they were training to go into Gaza, he was in a group of 16 guys who were essentially bodyguards of the brigadier general and the special equipment for all the paratroopers in Gaza. Technically, they were "safe," as they weren't on the frontline of battle, and other soldiers were assigned to protect these guys. Binyamin was frustrated that he wasn't fighting himself. At one point, the other Negevist got injured, so Binyamin was then given the Negev gun and was involved in the fighting.

They were stationed in northern Gaza. There was a house from which Hamas terrorists were shooting. The soldiers engaged them, but they weren't able to neutralize the terrorists from afar. One commander, Jamal Abbas, a Druze soldier, along with his right-hand man Shachar Friedman, said: "I'm going in – we just can't have the terrorists shooting at us and putting many soldiers in danger." Binyamin saw they were going in and he still had his Negev, and he said: "You need ammo. I am coming with you." He pushed his way in to join the soldiers. They got into the house, killing two terrorists, but one was hiding in the corner, and he killed all three of the IDF soldiers. It was typical of Binyamin to push his way forward – to take care of whatever needs to get done.

This was on Shabbat morning, November 18th. When were you informed that he had fallen?

That Shabbat morning, I was at shul (synagogue). Right after Torah reading I started feeling antsy and unable to stay. My ten-year-old daughter was surprised to see me going home, but I said I felt I had to go home and say Tehillim. **I was bawling and davening for a while – I didn't know what I was feeling.** I just told my daughter I wished everyone could be home for Shabbat together. My Chana sat there hugging me. She gave me *Sefer*

Mitzvat HaBitachon (The Mitzvah of Trusting God) and said, "I think you need this." We learned together, wiped my face and carried on. We got ready for lunch, and that afternoon we were taking a nap. My husband, who had been napping on the couch downstairs, woke me up and frantically said: "Get dressed and come downstairs." "Are the kids okay?" I asked him. "No," he said. I worried something happened to Chana, but why was it so quiet? No ambulance siren? As soon as I left my room and saw the soldiers at the staircase, I knew what that meant. I understood the phrase: "*Vayidom Aharon,* and Aharon was silent," when he learned of the death of his sons. There was nothing to say other than "*Baruch Dayan HaEmet.*" (Blessed be the true judge)

I asked them when he had fallen, and they told me the battle was between 9:30 and 10:30 in the morning – pretty much when I had left shul and came home. It was a shock, but on some level it wasn't.

It was surreal. Initially, we felt it was our personal tragedy but within a very short time we realized Binyamin's loss was a national one. Binyamin was the son/brother of the entire nation.

Many people attended the funeral. It was pouring rain. All we could see were the people in the front who we knew; we had no idea how many people were there, apparently there were many of whom we had never met. We knew it was live streamed for our family in the Diaspora, but only later learned that so many people we don't know from Israel and around the world also watched it. It was very personal to begin with, but as the *Shiva* was getting larger and larger, it dawned on me that you never know who is hearing you and watching you. Binyamin became someone people could connect with, a role model, and people want to learn from him and gain inspiration from him. Every step of the way he has reached hundreds and thousands more people; we never could have imagined that he would reach so many people. He was our Binyamin, but now he belongs to everyone, as every soldier does. I feel that way visiting other *Shivas* – these soldiers are all my soldiers, they are all our soldiers. Everyone feels this connection to them.

I was hesitant, but decided that I should speak at the *levaya* (funeral). I asked each person to take on one thing to try and improve themselves as a person to hasten the *Geulah* (redemption). People I never met were coming into the *Shiva* and signing up to commit – I was told one woman turned her whole kitchen kosher! I tend to be a positive person and try to help others and raise them up usually on a one-to-one basis, not with crowds. It's been different now. I think people have connected to me because I am a mother, and I speak from the heart – I am just going one day at a time, speaking to whichever person, group or community Hashem (God) brings our way.

You have become a source of strength for many others, but what gives you strength?

Firstly, I really feel and see that Hashem is constantly sending us hugs and kisses. Through all the pain of losing Binyamin, we are *zoche* (merit) to witness and experience so much of His *chessed* (kindness). I take great comfort in the verse, "*Shivtecha u'mishantecha heima yenachamuni,* Your rod and Your staff – they comfort me," that even when there is seemingly stricter judgment, I know that too all comes from Hashem and is part of our relationship. I take comfort knowing that He is watching out for me and is directly involved in every moment my life.

I also take great comfort seeing the thousands of people Binyamin is now effecting. People are striving to learn from him and grow because of him. It is the greatest comfort that – thousands of people are learning and taking things on in his memory and are literally becoming better people. He is part of bringing *Mashiach*. I really feel Binyamin is giving me the *koach* (strength) to keep going, and Hashem keeps sending me people to speak to. I see the growth of Am Yisrael. It's remarkable and a great comfort.

We cry virtually every day for him – when we see a new picture of him, when we hear something else that he accomplished or simply think of how much he's missed – but Rob and I have made a conscious decision not to ask *"Lama,* Why?", but *"Le'ma,* For what? What can we do now? How can we grow? How can we try to make good of this?"

There is no point in going down the dark road. We need to live life. That's what these soldiers are fighting for and even dying for. Yes, we have moments. We feel pain, we acknowledge it, and then we pick up and move forward. Binyamin wouldn't want it another way. He wants us to dance.

How do you want Binyamin to be remembered?

Binyamin was a magnet for all kinds of Jews, and had a way of bringing people in. One thing he loved doing was bringing people along to *Kabbalat Shabbat,* so one thing we want to do is to create a spiritual, emotional place for therapeutic recovery. There are so many soldiers who have become religiously aware and even inspired during this time, from wearing *tzitzit* to connecting to other elements of Judaism. Binyamin learned in the Hesder Tzfat Yeshiva. We plan to open a program there b'ezrat Hashem that can be a point of entry for them where they can heal in a religious context.

Binyamin's essence was also intertwined with *kedusha,* with holiness. He believed deeply in *kedushat haAretz,* the holiness of the Land of Israel, and that this holiness is intertwined with kedushat Am Yisrael, the holiness of the people of Israel. He really believed that we are fighting this war to enable Jews to be able to live all over Israel, and believed passionately in Jews moving to live here. He believed deeply in the gift of Eretz Yisrael.

You are speaking to communities around the world. what is your message to the Jewish people?

Part of Binyamin's legacy is that he really worked on himself and maximized his life, even if it was short. He accomplished in 21 years what might take a long lifetime for many others who are not focussed on their life mission. The message I hope he leaves is to inspire others to try and be their best self, and stay focused on their goals, of what's really important in life.

I really believe that each of our soldiers who have fallen in this war are working in heaven, building the Beit HaMikdash. It is our job, here in this world, to work on ourselves and keep our *Achdut* (unity) to be worthy to bring it down. To be *zoche* (merit) of the complete redemption."

BEIT BINYAMIN, a memorial for Binyamin offering respite, recovery and rejuvenation to those directly affected by the war.
beitbinyamin.org

STORIES OF OUR BELOVED AND HOLY HOSTAGES WHO FOUND GOD IN THE TERROR TUNNELS OF GAZA

For two years, the Jewish people, Christians and many others prayed intensely for the release of innocent people of all ages taken hostage, abducted on *Shemini Artzeret* and released two years later on *Hashanah Raba,* the day of salvation, celebrated right before *Shemini Atzeret* October 7th, the day that Hamas attacked the Jewish people.

Hostages taken by the terrorists in Gaza were ordinary secular people of all ages, from babies to elderly. Some were attending a music festival and others lived in nearby communities to Gaza. The majority of these hostages perished in the tunnels of Gaza. Today those surviving hostages are inspirational, famous and holy people shining light and love to the Jewish people and to the entire world. They have an important message for all of humanity.

President Trump said to some of the hostages when they were visiting the White House." You are no longer hostages, you are heroes". I think they are heroes because they were divinely chosen to fight in this historic battle between good and evil.

To me, the lives of the hostages were used for a holy purpose. They, alive and deceased, exposed the evil of Hamas for the world and also revealed the beauty and love of the Jewish people for each other. Every day, thousands of people gathered in Tel Aviv to pray for their release. Their captivity also brought hundreds of thousands of people all over the world into heartfelt prayer for their release. Many of those praying for the release of the hostages were inspired into making a commitment to become better people and do additional acts of kindness on their behalf to secure their release.

The stories of our beloved and holy hostages remind us once again that people can go through hell and come out transformed and shining. These hostages for the most part were awakened to the Divine Presence and grew in faith rather than be disillusioned during their tortuous captivity. Though starving, these hostages resisted all efforts to convert them to Islam, even when promised additional food and a more comfortable living situation.

Some of the hostages even fasted on Yom Kippur, even though they may not have fasted before. Being connected to God became the most primary way to survive. Many of the hostages became religiously observant because of what they endured in the tunnels. In these personal accounts of the hostages, the processes fortifying them during captivity are shared. May these stories inspire each of us when we face our own challenges in life.

I FELT THAT I WAS SURVIVING FOR A REASON.

Or Levy

Excerpts from an interview. Found on YouTube

Arrived at Nova Festival with wife at 6:28 am. Rockets began at 6:30 am.

We initially thought the rockets were fireworks. When it became clear what was really happening, we fled to a bomb shelter. There were 27 people in a shelter meant for four people. The terrorists were throwing grenades and we were throwing them back at them. Finally, they pulled me out and put me on a pick-up truck. I pleaded for my life. I have a son.

We passed through a mob of Gazans who wanted to murder us. I was more afraid of them than the Hamas terrorists. I was injured. They did medical treatment on me without anesthesia. I could not make any noise.

We were placed in an apartment. There was a radio there and we learned Arabic and learned that there were 250 hostages. We were not allowed to talk in the apartment. We whispered. I forget what the sound of my voice was. We had one meal a day. The apartment shook because rockets were fired close by. I always thought that death was possible any second.

I began to pray, but not really feel I was praying to God. I would think of all the things I would do if released. All the amends I would make for all the wrong things I did in life. One day, I was given an orange and then I was brought into the tunnels. In the tunnels we could talk and even laugh. Hersh told us "He who has a *why* to live can bear any *how*." We lived in the tunnels, chained together with big metal chains in pitch darkness. When one of us had to go to the bathroom, the others went with him. We ate one pita a day sharing a 1/2 can of chic peas. We were starving.

After October 7th, I became a big believer in God. I spoke to God, I did not speak to God before this time. I didn't really believe in God before. When I could feel I could not handle any more, I asked God to help us, to save us. Then something good happened. For example, I even got a cup of tea. I began to say *Shema Yisrael,* grateful that somehow I was still alive. I felt that I was surviving for a reason.

One day, one of the terrorists asked "Why do you Jews care about living?" He was not a young kid but a fifty year old man. They are fighting a holy war. They believe in death not in life. I saw that you cannot negotiate with them.

Then one day, Hamas removed the chains off our legs after wearing them for more than a year. We were told that thirty people would be released. We had to wait a week. That was the longest week ever. We were four hostages but only three of us would be released. We did not want to be very happy in front of the one remaining in captivity. We just prayed, feeling that still in any moment they could kill us.

Prior to my release, I was put on a stage before the world and told to say thank you to Hamas for keeping me alive. I was then taken to the Red Cross and then to the Israeli military. I immediately asked about my wife and told that she had been murdered. They then showed me a video of my son. It was the happiest day and most sad day.

When I left my son was two years old and now he is three and half years old. I wondered if my son would remember me. I promised myself that I would work hard to rebuild his trust.

My son remembered me. He ran to me, hugged me and asked me 'Why did it take so long to come to me'. He asked "where is Mommy". I cried and told him that Mommy is dead. I cried again. My son hugged me as to comfort me. He is my strength. We are now always together. We even sleep together.

I do not want to be sorry for myself. I want to be happy, even though I still mourn for my wife. But I am alive, I am here. This is my victory.

If a person gets stronger through rough times, he will thrive. This is what I learned. The Jewish people know this. We went through the holocaust, so much persecution, but we thrived as a people.

When we get all the hostages out, the Jewish people will thrive again.

I give talks now to give hope to people and to bring my brothers and sisters home. I know the remaining hostages are going through a living hell. I feel salvation personally but I cannot really recover until everyone is home. *Am Yisrael Chai*. We really feel this. I am grateful for all the love shown to me.

EXCERPTS FROM INTERVIEW WITH SAPIR COHEN AT BEIT TEFILLAH ARIZONA GALA

Sapir Cohen

Hostage in Gaza for 55 days

I am happy. Before being taken captive, I felt something bad would happen to me. I went to many doctors. One doctor told me that I have virus in my body but it is not dangerous. I read something that if a person says this chapter of psalms (27) for 30 days, all will be well. I did not fully understand the importance of the message of this psalm until I was held captive in Gaza.

From the moment that terrorists came into the kibbutz, I understood the meaning of psalm more. I kept repeating the psalm over and over and I felt peace. The terrorist broke into the house that my boyfriend and I were hiding and took both of us into Gaza.

I knew that this can't be in the end. As I was paraded around in Gaza, the Gazans who saw me wanted to beat me. I knew that the goal was to take people alive. Every day felt like a miracle in the tunnels. I understood I was supposed to be there. I was next to a young girl who was very frightened. I knew I was there to make her happy and feel safe.

I kept repeating psalm 27th. I continually say, **"Thank you God because you can help me and this young girl. Thank you angels." Later I understood that there were so many people who prayed for me, who also became better people because of me. They were my angels.**

In the first two weeks of captivity, my parents did not know if I was killed or if I was still alive. My parents began to hold gatherings. People would arrive feeling sad but my parents would tell everyone. I want every one attending to be happy and dance and send positive energy to my daughter. My parents always taught me that we can always choose to be happy in terrible circumstances.

It is important for me to tell my story and connect with Jews all over the world. I meet many good people. These people give me power to continue.

Since the experience of Gaza, Sapir began to keep Shabbat. "**I told God I will keep Shabbat from the very moment the terrorists entered the door to capture me and my boyfriend. Shabbat makes me feel peace and makes me feel free.**

When asked what is your hope for the future? Sapir answered "in one of the tunnels I was able to watch television and I saw all the demonstrations held to release hostages. I came to believe that when the Jewish people are united, they will be very strong and defeat all our enemies. I am hoping and praying that the Jews will be united and be together very soon."

EVERY DAY I THANKED GOD FOR BEING ALIVE

Omer Shem Tov

Excepts from television interviews
with Fox 10 Phoenix with John Kook

Omer Shem Tov was 23 years old when captured at the Nova Festival and held hostage for 505 days. The first 53 days of being held he was with two friends and moved frequently to different apartments.

Omer was separated from his friends and held in a little cell that did not allow him to stand up or even stretch his arms. He was starved, and tortured mentally and physically. The terrorists would curse him, telling him that his family has forgotten about him.

He was locked in this cell alone for 50 days in pitch darkness.

While sitting in total darkness, Omer began to experience the light and love of the Divine Presence. He was alone with God. He talked to God from the depth of his soul. Even though he could not tell if it was morning or night, when he would wake up from sleep, he would say the traditional Jewish prayer expressing gratitude for waking up. **"Whenever I felt sad or depressed, I talked to God. God gave me strength."**

Omer tried his best to be helpful and friendly to the terrorists. They accepted his offer to do whatever he could to help them. He cooked for them, he cleaned for them, and he dug tunnels and did electrical work, whatever he could do to be helpful, he did. He learned Arabic after five months of captivity but never revealed this ability to his captives. He heard them boasting about how they raped women in the tunnels, and murdered other hostages because when were simply tired of seeing them.

Omer spoke "**Every day my faith in God got stronger. I**

always believed that I would go home. I would see my parents, we are hugging, and so happy that I have been released. Every day I thanked God for being alive. I thanked God for whatever food I had been given." Omer was given a small biscuit and a little salty water daily. The practice of gratitude for everything, even his breath, helped fortify his faith.

His grandmother has given him a red string, known to offer protection and blessing according to Kabbalistic teachings. The string usually lasts on the wrist for a month or six weeks. His red string lasted up to his entire captivity and broke right before his release. Omer has had a red string now tattooed on his wrist.

Five months before his release, a television was brought into the tunnel and he saw for the first time the protests in Israel taking place every Saturday for the release of hostages. Omer then became aware of all that is being done for the hostages. He wondered what his parents were doing to secure his release as he did not see them on television.

When Donald Trump was elected president, the terrorists were unhappy; they were openly rooting for the election of Kamala Harris. After Trump's election, the terrorists started to treat the hostages better. There was a noticeable change in their treatment to him.

Prior to his release, the terrorists started to give him more food, so he would look better when he was released. Omer was released with two other hostages. He spoke that he was shocked upon his release. He was greeted by a female officer. He asked her for a hug as he had not been shown any love or affection for more than a year. It was a beautiful hug. He was asked what he would like. He said a burger. When he was transported to the hospital he was greeted with 1000 burgers that people donated to him. He happily distributed them to everyone.

After nine days after his release, Omer had the privilege to meet

President Trump who was instrumental in securing his release. Since his release Omer is totally dedicated to working for the release of the remaining 53 hostages. Only 20 of them may be alive.

When asked about the impact of the hostage experience had on him." **I am stronger, I am a better man. I am confident, I can do everything. God put me in this situation for a reason. I am more focused and living with greater clarity as to my purpose in life. I am grateful."**

Omer went on to say. "The Jewish people are not whole because of the hostages. We can't resume living a normal life while our brothers and sisters are in the hell of captivity."

His message to the world. " **We are living through miracles every day. Let's not take life for granted."**

Omer Shem Tov, Hostage in tunnels of Gaza for 505 days.
These are excepts from interviews in America after his release.

CHAPTER 5

WHAT DOES IT MEAN TO TRUST IN GOD

Mendel Kalmenson's book *Positivity Bias* shares a foundational teaching from the Lubavitcher Rebbe on the crucial distinction between faith and trust.

"What is the difference between *Emunah* (faith) and *Bitachon* (trust)?" the Rebbe was asked. He responded that *Bitachon* is not simply a higher form of *Emunah*; it's a completely different way of relating to God. "If one is faced with a problem and has *Emunah*," he explained, "one has **faith** that God will help him overcome his problems. But if one has *Bitachon*, one does not think there is a problem at all, for he understands that God does not send problems, only **challenges**."

Someone who truly trusts in God's goodness doesn't see obstacles, only opportunities for growth, divine connection, and blessing. In the midst of trial, faith and trust is an important decision a person must make to not only survive, but to grow and thrive.

The Lubavitcher Rebbe emphasized the importance of trust in God in a strong way:

> **"Let us trust in God with the confidence that everything will turn out for the best, for that very trust brings about the positive outcome."**

This message is even stronger than just positive thinking.

HOW DOES TRUSTING IN GOD MAKE A DIFFERENCE

Trusting in God becomes especially important and beneficial when we face the inevitable challenges of life. Trusting in God offers us protection and blessing. It can even change our fate. Rebbe Nachman of Breslov taught that trusting in God creates a vessel enabling us to receive directly from God. Our consciousness is changed from fear and anxiety to one of receptivity and confidence.

Ibn Paquda in his book *Duties of the Heart* provides a powerful example of the power of trusting in God: A person who owns a store but isn't selling his wares. He knows that God will protect him and manage his affairs better than he could on his own. If money doesn't come in one way, it will come in another. The trusting God person is not anxious and knows he will receive his livelihood without much trial or struggle. Because he is not anxious and trusts in God, he easily attracts opportunities for increased livelihood.

Some think that what they have is due solely to their own efforts. This is the voice of the ego within us which believes that it is in charge of reality. We can easily feel desperate if we believe that we have to do everything on our own. The deeper truth is that God is in charge and blesses us with what we need to fulfill our soul purpose. Trust in God opens the gate for blessing in our lives. We become peaceful, loving and accepting when we are trusting and aligned with God.

Similarly, this is even true in regards to our health. I have heard of many stories of people who received a frightening diagnosis from a doctor but went on to heal and live beautiful productive lives because they trusted in God. There are even such stories in this book.

When we are ill, and we trust in God, we trust that healing will happen for us, even if we are not cured in the way we expect or want. Judaism teaches that the body receives its spiritual nourishment from the soul through its good thoughts, feelings and actions. The body cannot function if not for the life force energy of the soul. It is the soul that gives the eyes the capacity to see, the ears the capacity to hear, the nose the capacity to smell, etc. When the body and soul enjoy the proper partnership, a person is well. When we nourish our soul, strengthen our divine connection, relax and trust, we draw healing upon us.

Relaxation is very important in healing. Trust in God allows us to relax. Whether we work with conventional or alternative modalities for healing, we must always remember that God is our ultimate healer. Trust always in God for your ultimate healing. Strengthen faith and trust in God. You are not alone. Pray for your healing and that of others. It makes a difference.

Ibn Paquda teaches us that if we do not put our trust in God, we will put our trust elsewhere. And God will abandon us to the power that we trust. Now this is frightening! If we choose to live our lives not aligned with Divine Will, God will also allow us to do so. The Torah offers the following example. Before entering the land of Israel, the leaders of the tribes went to spy on the land prior to entering, even though they knew that it was divine will that the Jewish people reside in the land of Israel Ten of the leaders expressed fear of entering the land of Israel. Consequently, God answered their cries. They were denied entry into the land and died in the desert. Only the two spies, Caleb and Yehoshua, who were not afraid, lived and entered the land.

Furthermore, Ibn Paquda reminds us that we will ultimately be unable to sustain what we build in our lives unless we fortify ourselves with faith and align with Divine Will. *Duties of the Heart* book spends considerable time explaining to us why we can only trust in God and not in anything else. When we trust, God will send the right angels to protect, care and bless us in times of crisis. When we trust in God, we stop feeling like victims. We do not blame ourselves nor do we blame other people. Who we are as people is also not diminished when others blame us for their unhappiness. Everyone has their own soul journey. We trust that God is charge of our life and that of others.

The Rebbe Rabbi Nachman of Breslov told us that the reward for not taking things personally is that our prayers are answered. Taking what people say personally only weakens our connection with God and to ourselves. Often, people project their own shortcomings onto other people rather than take responsibility for what has been triggered within them. We must always be mindful to take responsibility for what has been triggered within our relationships.

When we accept that everything is happening in our lives

according to the divine plan, we know that there will be ultimately goodness and blessing in our lives. This realization helps us to let go of the need for anxiety and quiets the chatter on the part of our ego attempting to manipulate others or seek their approval to secure our safety and success. Trust in God reminds us that we do not have to give ourselves up to feel safe or get ahead in life. We also not need praise or approval from others.

Trusting in God is also important because it frees us from the feeling that we need to be somewhere else in life to fulfill our purpose. We are exactly where we are meant to be. When we are supposed to be somewhere else, we will be guided to be there. Divine providence is always at play in the lives of people who trust in God.

Our true security and our self- worth only comes from our relationship with God. While others may serve as agents of blessing for us, the blessing itself always originates from God and is dependent on our capacity to receive. What is most important for us is to strengthen our vessels to receive what God wants to give us, whatever it is, whether it feels good or challenging. When we stop trying to figure out life, stop fighting with life and stop seeking to control life, we can then access our soul and open to receive the love, and support God wants to give us.

When the chatter of ego mind finally becomes quiet, when we focus on what is really present for us, we are naturally drawn to what is true, real, and peaceful. We enter a state I describe as holy silence. This state of holy silence increases our awareness to the heightened vibrations of our own holy precious soul and her guidance.

Our very soul is the flame of divine light shining within our body temple. All feelings of desperation or victimhood are easily relinquished when we are bathing in the love and wisdom of our own soul and deeper awareness of the reality of God. We are not here on our own. God is within us and with us. And God is the foundation of all life on this planet.

When we access our own soul, our current relationships with others are also deepened and people more aligned with our soul purpose enter our lives. New ways to be of service to others are also revealed to us. This brings greater blessings of love and joy into our lives.

MEDITATION ON THE DIVINE SOUL

Begin by being aware of the breath for a few minutes until the mind becomes more quiet. With every breath repeat "God breathes into me a pure soul." The soul is the essence of who we really are.

As you inhale, God is breathing into your physical body the life force energy of the soul to enliven the body and make all the organs function. This level of your soul is known as the ***nefesh***. The seat of the *nefesh* is the liver. Say the word *nefesh* to yourself. Take a few breaths to marvel on how all the physical organs in the body function so marvelously, even when you are not mindful of them. This physical body is a temple for your soul. "**My body is a holy temple For Divine Light and Love.**" Meditate on this affirmation.

The body and soul are partners for a brief period of time enabling the other to express our soul potential. The soul needs the body. For the body is a vehicle for the soul to reside in this physical world. The body needs the soul to elevate and purify it. Affirm to take care of your physical body with the attention and respect due it.

Now become aware of the emotional body, seated in the heart. God is breathing into you a more refined level of soul known as ***ruach***. *Ruach* gives us the capacity to feel, to love, to feel compassion and strength. The soul loves to feel deeply. So give yourself permission to feel. Breathe into the heart center and open the heart to receive the divine breath of *ruach.* Allow yourself to be with whatever feelings are present in the emotional body. Open the heart to receive and radiate the divine *ruach* energies of love and compassion. You can repeat the word *ruach* silently to be more aware of this flow of soul energy in the heart.

Now become aware of the top of the head, the seat of the level of soul known as ***neshama,*** the higher self, the inner knowing, giving us the capacity to perceive Godliness. This is the seat of our intuition. Some of us will even begin to feel energy around the top of the head. That is good.

We can experience the energies of the crown of the personal sovereignty of the soul. This is the essential you. This part of you was present in your childhood, and in your adult life, in the bad times and good times. The *neshama* is unaffected by what is happening outside of you and even within you. Repeat the word *neshama* to increase awareness of this level of your being.

Become aware that there is energy surrounding the body. The energy surrounding the body is known as ***Chaya*** and ***Yehida.*** On these levels of the soul, we are most connected to the Divine.

So expanded, this level of our soul does not fit into the physical body. This level of the soul surrounds the body. This may be likened to the aura. The level of soul known as *chaya* is the level of Divine Will and vision connecting the *neshama* level to the highest level known as *yehida.* The level of soul known as *yehida* is the inner spiritual essence, that is, one with the Divine. On this level we are an actual part of the Divine. There is no separation. Affirm that "My soul is a part of God.' Meditate on this affirmation.

The soul is inside our physical body and also outside of our physical body. Our essential identity is that of the pure soul inhabiting and also enlivening the physical body.

As you inhale, feel the divine soul's desire to ascend, to transcend the body and unify completely with God. Climb in your awareness from *nefesh* to *ruach* to *neshama*, to *chaya* to *yehida*. Stay in the space after the inhalation as long as you can comfortably for this is a place of great quiet and peace.

As you exhale, travel back in the other direction, return to this physical world. Be aware that the pure soul is now returning and re-entering the physical body. Return in your awareness from *yehida* to *chaya* to *neshama* to *ruach* to *nefesh*. Rest and internalize what you received in the space between the breaths.

I find it helpful at times to employ and meditate on the letters of the Divine Name YHVH to correspond to the levels of the soul. *Nefesh* is Hay, *Ruach* is Vav, *Neshama* is Hay, and *Chaya* and *Yehida* is Yud.

To intensify the awareness of the soul, light a candle for gazing. Imagine that your body is a candle and the soul is the flame. Feel that the flame of your soul burns brightly because it truly does.

Alternate between gazing at the candle in front of you and closing your eyes and visualizing yourself as a candle. The various colors in the flame are said in kabbalah teachings to correspond to the levels of the soul. *Nefesh* is the black light. *Ruach* is the white light. *Neshama* is the yellow light surrounding the white light. *Chaya* is the blue light. When you gaze at the candlelight, allow the light of the candle to fill your entire vision.

Meditating on the light of the candle offers us an entrance to the light of the Holy Temple, the light of Shabbos, the light of creation, and to the light of our own soul. When gazing on a candle, take time to **listen to light**. There is a message for you to receive right now. Listen to the voice of the soul within you. What does your soul need to fulfill its mission, its purpose for being in this world?

"**The soul of man is the candle of God**" Your soul is the flame of God. Your body is the candle. This is not a metaphor but a description of who you are.

Like the flame of a candle, the soul is transcendent, rising, flickering, dancing upward. The light of your soul is shining brightly. Awareness of the light of the soul burns away negativities and impurities within you and outside of you. The more you let go, the brighter the light of your soul shines.

This healing light of the soul transforms challenges and trials to spiritual opportunities, empowering you to shine, even more brightly than before the onset of the challenges and trials.

CHAPTER 6

TRUST IN GOD IS INTEGRAL TO OUR SOUL PURPOSE

To understand why trust is so integral to our soul purpose, we can turn to the mystical teachings of Rabbi Yitzchak Luria. He explains that before there was time and space, there was only *Ain Sof*, Limitless Light. A desire arose within this infinite existence: to bestow love and to be known. *Ain Sof* then performed an act of *Tzimtzum*, or divine contraction. *Ain Sof* withdrew its infinite light to create a void, a space for a finite world to exist within it.

This is a critical point: creation was not an act of revelation, but of concealment. The Divine Name used in the Genesis creation story, *Elohim*, is associated with *Gevurah*, the divine attribute of boundaries and limitation. God's light had to be veiled in order to create our world.

The ultimate purpose of creation is fulfilled in our dense and challenging physical world. In this physical world, the light of *Ain Sof* is most hidden, most concealed. We were placed here in this physical world because concealment provides the greatest opportunity for God to bestow goodness and, in turn, to be known and loved by beings who experience themselves as separate from God.

Being human offers our soul opportunities that don't exist in the higher, more unified spiritual planes. It is such a gift to be physically embodied, even with all the challenges we face being human. We suffer in life when we forget that we are spiritual beings and we identify only with our physical bodies. When our physicality is our primary identification, it's easy to feel that God is distant or absent, especially during hardship.

Though our time in this physical world is temporary, we foolishly devote so much energy and time to fortifying our sense of ego identity, rather than be guided and uplifted by the wisdom of our own soul. Our soul is our truest essence which existed before this life and will continue to exist when we are no longer physically embodied.

Too often, we try to accomplish so much because of the desires of the ego. We want to be recognized, we want to be loved, we want material success and we want to feel safe. Ultimately these pursuits will not fulfill us if they are not connected to our soul purpose. The deeper truth is that when we define ourselves by our worldly accomplishments, we are actually invalidating ourselves on a soul level. Strengthening our ego identity, no matter how successful we may become, is no replacement for soul embodiment and divine connection. It seems to make sense and behooves us to invest time and energy in what will last beyond this physical world.

Our soul is always a part of God, no matter what happens to our physical or emotional bodies. The soul is patiently waiting for us to access the inner wisdom and the deeper truth that God is always animating and guiding our existence. When we wake up to this deeper truth, we transform our challenges into spiritual opportunities and blessings.

In time, we may come to appreciate that the challenges we

face are often part of a "soul agreement" made before our physical embodiment and have been designed specifically as opportunities to enable us to fulfill our soul's mission for this physical embodiment. They were supposed to happen as they did. Nothing is random.

The human experience is supposed to be challenging. Life is designed in such a way that we will eventually at times all need to cry out to God from a place of pain and open to a more expanded consciousness. Our pain awakens us to heed the call to go beyond what we previously know. To become whole, our hearts must break. Otherwise, we might fall into the arrogance of believing we are the sole authors of our lives.

When your heart breaks, remember the deep teaching: "There is nothing as whole as a broken heart." It is the crack that lets the divine light and love enter more fully. The challenges we face are custom-designed to help us fulfill our soul destiny. Trusting that everything happening is for our ultimate good changes our fate and ironically empowers us to live more fully.

Our prayers may not be answered in the time and way we want. Nevertheless, sincere prayer is always answered, because its primary purpose is to open gateways to experience closeness with God. This closeness is the greatest gift and it is our ultimate purpose in life. Our trust in God is particularly rewarded when we are challenged.

When we truly trust in God, when we access our pure holy soul, our entire experience of life is transformed. Do not give up when prayers are not answered immediately as requested. God's timetable of what is best for us is usually different than ours. To fulfill our soul purpose, we often need to go through a period of purification and refinement so we become a vessel capable of embodying the more intense vibrations of love and light needed to fulfill our soul purpose. Patience is important.

Like the caterpillar that has to shed its skin in order to fulfill its destiny to become a butterfly, similarly, we have to let go of limiting ideas of who we think we are and what we feel we are capable of being. It may not be easy to let go of what has made us feel previously safe and comfortable. But holding on to what is known does not necessarily make us safe. We do not actualize our soul purpose in life by playing it safe, by being comfortable, by being defensive or by engaging in feelings of victimhood and old habitual patterns that do not empower us to be live purposefully and joyfully.

Questions to be asked and meditated upon:

Am I willing to let go of what has limited me and open to be more of who my soul wants me to embody in this time in my life?
Say Yes to yourself and to life silently and out loud.

Am I willing to let go of regrets of the past and concerns of the future and be grateful to receive the blessings of being alive in the present moment?
Say Yes to yourself silently and out loud.

Am I willing to accept that all has unfolded so as to empower me to better fulfill my soul purpose and do something of service for others?
Say Yes to yourself silently and out loud.
And then – Amen.

HEALING THE PAST TO TRUST THE PRESENT

For many, it is hard to trust in God because we did not feel safe or loved as children. Our parents are God's first representatives. In infancy, we learn whether the world is a safe place or not. If our cries went unanswered, we may have learned that our needs do not matter. Consequently, we learned to abandon our authentic selves to please others for survival; a pattern that can persist for a lifetime, leaving us feeling lonely and isolated as adults as well, especially if we experienced terrible abuse in our childhood.

To heal these early childhood wounds, we need to learn to reparent ourselves. By listening deeply and compassionately to our own hearts, we can heal the wounded parts of ourselves filled with judgment, fear, and doubt. Within the heart of each of us remains the inner child who needs our love and compassion.

This inner child is calling out for our love and not for criticism. We often need to engage in sweet talk to ourselves as a daily practice or whenever we are hurting. As adults, we can and must learn to love and accept ourselves as we are. The daily practice of self-love is foundational preparation to our soul awakening.

When we accept and embrace our own vulnerability, we naturally become more open to experiencing the unconditional love of God. It is important to appreciate that **we are not defined by the wounds of our past unless we choose to be.** Our pain served a purpose for us to deepen our yearning for connection with God and also with ourselves in a new way. This compassionate awareness supports us in going forward in our lives in new, more expanded ways.

For many of us, it may be helpful to seek individual and group counseling, or spiritual guidance at varying times of challenge. The meditations in this book will also help to heal early wounding.

MEDITATION ON THE INNER CHILD AND LOVE

Assume a comfortable seated position on the floor or in a chair. If you prefer, you may lie on your back, provided you are sure that you will not fall asleep.

Allow your eyes to close. Focus on the breath, the inhalation and exhalation for a few minutes. With each exhalation, allow yourself to go deep inside. It is safe to go deep inside oneself. Travel in your awareness to the most intimate place within yourself, a secret place within where only you can go.

In this meditation, you will have an opportunity to review the descent of your soul into this physical world, so as to review early decisions you made about God and yourself. Many of these early decisions are no longer appropriate. God willing, this reflection will be one of healing and letting go of limiting and false ideas of who you are and who God is.

Imagine that you can go back to the time of your birth. Torah teaches us that at the time of your parent's engagement or when your parents decided to come together, you looked down from the place of souls in the spiritual world and chose these parents or they were chosen for you as well as the circumstances of your birth. Why were you attracted to these particular individuals as your parents?

Visualize your parents as the people they were at the time of your conception. What was their consciousness at that time? Were they ready for you? Did they wait a long time for you? Or did you come unexpectedly? Were they happy about your arrival?

Now, see yourself in the secure physical place called the womb, where all your needs were met. Imagine yourself floating in warm water, safe and secure. Your soul gradually became accustomed to being joined to a body. It is said that during the nine months of gestation the infant learns Torah. We know what we are supposed to do in this world. The memories are there. Often we learn something new and we feel that we knew it before.

After nine months of being nurtured in this way, we are forced to leave and enter directly into the physical world. Your birth was a great miracle. Your parents may have been conduits, instruments for God, but God is your true parent. You now share in the mystery of life just as your parents do. You are a child of God. Your parents are also children of God.

Yet, you, as an infant, are now a little closer to God. You are so pure and innocent. You are absorbed and fascinated by the sensation of being in a physical body. God made you so sweet, so alive, so helpless. Your parents loved you as much as they possibly could. As an infant, you are totally dependent. You have so many needs, you have such a big need to be loved and held. You also need to be fed and to be changed. You needed a lot of attention.

When you expressed your needs and you cried, did your parents respond quickly or did you wait a long time for your basic needs to be met? Did you share your parent's attention with siblings? Were they close in age to you? What was your relationship with siblings like when you were young and today? Did any of your siblings take care of you? Did your parents play with you a lot? Or do you remember being left for long periods of time in a playpen or crib? Were you the center of their lives?

Now see yourself, as the child you once were, so eager to play, to laugh, to love and enjoy life. Recall some experiences when you felt particularly playful and lovable as a child. This playful child lives within you today. Do you give your inner child time to play?

There were also times when you, as a child or infant, were hurt, when you were frightened, when you wanted to be held and no one was there. You may have been told that it was not okay to be who you were. You needed to behave in a certain way to be loved. You may have been told to not feel the feelings that you felt. You may even have been hit or beaten. You may have felt that you were not a good boy or girl or that you were not really wanted. You may even have felt responsible for your parent's pain or for any conflict between your parents.

Sometimes, you felt so bad that you cried and were told that you should not cry. Or you cried and were ignored. No one came to comfort you. Take time to reflect.

What happens to your tears today? Are your needs met? Take time to listen to the child within. Ask your inner child to speak to you now. "What do you need little one?" Assure your inner child that you are now an adult and that you will take care of him or her. Tell your inner child that he does not have to pretend to be someone he is not before you. Tell your inner child that he is lovable, sweet, and beautiful.

Say the following several times silently and then out loud. "You (your name) are lovable and I am there for you. I will do the best I can to take care of you." Say it until you are sure that your inner child believes you.

Then repeat silently to your inner child, "You are lovable and God is there for you." Or "I love you unconditionally." Tell this inner child that there is nothing he could do that would make him unlovable. Be the voice of unconditional love for your inner child. Remember that God created this world for love. Your child knows how to love and receive love. What would God say to this inner child?

Imagine that you can see a movie of how love has unfolded in your life so far? Recall acts of love done for you and acts of love you performed for others. Recall people with whom you have loved. Reflect on the gifts and growth opportunities these relationships provided. Do these people have anything in common? Do you notice any patterns? Have you been betrayed or hurt by love? What have you learned about love and your capacity to love? Were you more concerned about what you received from others than what you gave?

Go to the present moment. Are you presently open to increasing and opening love in your life? How large is your circle of love and caring? How intimate? How would you like to increase your capacity to love? What can you do to begin opening to love in your life now?

When you finish reflecting, you can take time to journal about these questions and meditation or talk to a close friend about the awareness you received during this meditation.

CHAPTER 7

HOW DO WE CULTIVATE AND DEEPEN TRUST IN GOD

Our trust and faith in God must not be dependent on our requests being fulfilled. If our relationship with God is transactional – if we see God as a cosmic force to be bribed or appeased- we are bound to be disappointed. This immature perception will make it impossible to trust God when life becomes difficult.

I once had a meditation student who prayed intensely for her son's recovery from a serious illness. When he passed away, she decisively terminated her relationship with God. In her mind, God could have answered her prayers but chose not to. This was unfortunate, because a deeper relationship with God could have offered her immense consolation, but her anger was too great. She loved the relaxation of meditation but couldn't tolerate the mention of God, whom she referred to only as "the G-word."

Her story illustrates a common crisis of faith. How do we trust God in the face of our personal trials or unmitigated evil in the world? Others may wonder how to transform feelings of emptiness and lingering feelings of sadness, in spite of a wonderful marriage and financial prosperity. The answer lies to both of these questions in addressing the needs of the soul on a daily basis.

It is crucial to know and understand that trusting in God does not mean being passive. Surrender is not resignation. To do nothing and expect God to provide is considered an act of rebellion. We must not place ourselves in dangerous situations and assume God will protect us. We must always do our best to meet our needs and share what God has given us while simultaneously trusting God to guide our efforts. Trust and action are partners. As we move deeper in our connection with God, we become channels of blessings for ourselves and others.

RECOMMENDATIONS TO CULTIVATE AND DEEPEN TRUST IN GOD

STEP ONE: START A CONVERSATION WITH GOD

One of the most direct ways to transform our relationship with God is to talk to God. This practice of talking to God can be done at a separate time or during the course of the day. There are thousands of Jews who are committed to doing this practice for one hour each day. Rabbi Nachman of Breslov attributed much of his elevated consciousness to this simple practice. If you want to take this on as a spiritual practice, begin by allowing 10-15 minutes for this practice. If you feel that there are no more words to say, sit in silence with the consciousness that God is before you. The words that you speak are for your benefit.

Share your heart; your pain, your doubts, your fears, your needs. Speak to God in your own words. My teacher, Reb Shlomo Carlebach, recommended whispering rather than talking. Find time each day for this sacred conversation. It is recommended that you speak out loud rather than just thinking.

Even if you doubt God is listening or even if there is a God, you can speak about your non-belief. This act itself changes you.

Talk to God as God is your best friend. Tell God all that is happening in your life, your challenges, and hardships. Know that God is the friend who never leaves you. God is there for you in good times and hard times. Ask God for the healing and comfort you need.

God knows who you are and what you really need. If you are not experiencing the Divine Presence, ask God sincerely from the depths of your heart to enter your life so you actually feel God's presence. You can and must be real with God. Ask God for the love and support to grow through the pain you may now be experiencing. Always take time to be quiet and listen to what is rising within your own heart and soul. If it is hard to you to talk to God, ask God to help you. Tell God that your life has no meaning if you do not experience being connected to God.

Connect then with the deep desire to align your personal will with Divine Will, to want what God wants for you. It is good to sit with this question. **What does God want of me at this time?**

In addition to talking to God for your needs, take time to pray for others, pray for the Jewish people, and pray for the people in your country, pray for the people in the entire world to wake up to the deeper truth of God and that of divine love.

Make it a practice to engage in a conversation with God, more than with people. This conversation can be long or short and take place at any time. If it feels important or it would be helpful, talk to people about God, not as a missionary, but only to share your experience with God as a way to transmit love and inspiration to them.

There are more expanded instructions for this meditation on talking to God at the end of this chapter.

STEP TWO: ADDRESS THE NEEDS OF THE SOUL

We can raise our spiritual energy and connect with our soul in countless ways:

- Prayer, meditation, spiritual or religious practice on a daily basis: Take on or deepen a spiritual or religious practice you are currently doing. Seek guidance if needed to begin. Make an effort to be consistent in whatever you choose to do.

- Perform good deeds: Perform acts of kindness to others, especially if they cannot do anything back for you. If you have time, volunteer to help another person or others. This is actually a spiritual gift you give to yourself.
- Spiritual learning: Continue to learn about the nature of God and divine service daily. Study the Bible and teachings about the Bible. This Bible and its commentaries are written to be studied and read numerous times. Read books written by holy people.
- Pray with a Jewish prayer book. Everything a person needs to learn about God and growing in consciousness and freedom can be found in the Jewish prayer book. Repeat at least two psalms daily.
- Engage in a creative pursuit such as writing, painting, dancing, playing or listening to music, etc.
- Spend time in nature as much as you can.
- Engage in mindful physical movement like yoga or Tai Chi or even walking daily.
- Practice the meditations, meditate on the affirmations and teachings in this book.

Each of us will be guided toward the practices that best support our healing and heightening of our resilience. The key is to actively and continually choose connection over victimhood, so we don't block the flow of blessing into our lives. Be sure that you nurture yourself with a few of these activities daily and most of them weekly or bi-weekly. Even a practice of 15 minutes to one hour each day will transform your life so as to receive healing and blessing.

STEP THREE: STRENGTHEN LOVING RELATIONSHIPS

Many stories of people in this book were helped to leave unbearable situations that they were unable to leave on their own by loving family and friends. When we trust in God, when we call out for help and cry holy tears, when we reach out to others, God sends the right people (angels) to help us. When we help others, we become the hands and feet of God and we are also filled with love and light. Giving to others is a privilege and the most powerful way to receive blessing in life.

Receiving and giving is a blessing. Reach out to connect with others when you need help and would benefit from connection and be willing to be present for others when they reach out to you as well. Every day, there are opportunities to give to others in small and large ways. Our giving to others must be without expectation of receiving something in return. God rewards all acts of self-less giving to others.

STEP FOUR: A DAILY PRACTICE OF GRATITUDE

The practice of gratitude opens the doorway to greater blessings. When we are grateful, we will be given greater insight and more experiences that will engender gratitude. Being grateful does not negate the pain we may experience but it does open us to receive love and blessing in life. We are blessed when we can be grateful for the awesome gift of being alive, moment to moment, as we are right now.

Even in the worst of times, there is always something to be grateful for. We can always be grateful, even for the gift of breath itself. "God is breathing and sustaining me with every breath."

In the course of the day, be mindful and grateful of experiences of divine synchronicity, blessings and protection experienced during the course of each day. At the end of the day, take a few moments to review the day and be grateful for the gifts received each day. Many people find that the practice of writing in a gratitude journal to be fortifying and inspirational.

As our practice of gratitude deepens, we even begin to reflect and appreciate the blessings that have taken place within us during times of challenge and how they impacted in shaping the people we became. We may even begin to feel grateful for the challenges we will face in the future and how we will continue to grow to become more divinely connected and embodied.

Gratitude can be practiced at any time of day. It is interesting to know that hundreds of thousands of Jews will wash their hands upon awakening and say blessings to greet the new day with gratitude. I find this also an important practice before greeting the day. We wash our hands in a special way, we say a few blessings, like the one for blessing our hands before engaging in a holy action, we say the blessing for awakening from sleep and greeting the new day and we say the Shema, the daily prayer affirming Divine Oneness. If you do not know how to do this, it will be easy to find guidance from rabbis and others in learning how to do this powerful daily practice.

STEP FIVE: FORGIVENESS AS A DAILY PRACTICE

Seeking and offering forgiveness is very important. There is even a nightly prayer in the Jewish prayer book to ask for forgiveness each night before bed. We are encouraged to take time nightly to review our day and forgive everyone, children, parents, friends, forgive everyone who impacted negatively on your life each day. We do this for others but mostly for ourselves. Holding on to anger blocks the flow of blessing in life. Most importantly, we also need to forgive ourselves for not being perfect, and for being too critical and judgmental toward ourselves and others.

"I hereby forgive anyone who angered or antagonized me or who sinned against me, whether against my body, my property, my house, against anything of mind, whether done accidentally, willfully, carelessly or purposefully. Whether through speech, deed, thought, or notion, whether in this transmigration or another transmigration. May no one be punished because of me. (ArtScroll Bedtime *Shema* prayer, page 319)

After forgiving others and ourselves, we need to practice blessing. Bless all your loved ones in speech and consider acts of kindness you can do for them and others during your waking hours.

GUIDED MEDITATION:
A CONVERSATION WITH GOD

Preparation

Find a quiet space where you can be undisturbed. Sit comfortably and take a few deep breaths to center yourself. We are advised to speak out loud and not stay just in our thoughts, particularly in the beginning of our conversation. There are three stages that we may experience in this meditative practice.

The Conversation (For Five To 60 Minutes)

1. BEGIN SPEAKING TO GOD AS YOU WOULD YOUR MOST TRUSTED FRIEND.

Tell God everything that is happening in your life; your challenges, your hardships, your joys. Know that God is the friend who never leaves you. Ask God to enter your life, to provide the healing and comfort you need.

- If you are angry, express your anger. You can be real with God. But ultimately, ask for the love and support to grow through your pain and challenges.
- Plead if you must. Tell God that you need to be in connection with God. Your life feels empty and is empty without this connection. Surrender your burdens and let God be active in your life.
- Ask God to help you release the hold that negative thoughts, negative emotions and even uncomfortable physical symptoms, have in your consciousness. Know that whatever is limiting or painful to

you does not define who you are. You are not a victim. You are not your illness. You are not your negativity nor your pain. Be gentle with yourself.

- Always take time to be vulnerable before the Holy One, the Creator of all of life. Reconnect with the natural, childlike faith that lies within us all. You are loved as you are right now. Hug yourself if it would be helpful to you. Everything that has happened to you has been for your growth and healing in this life time and for the next world. Make an effort to raise your consciousness to appreciate the growth and learning inspired by your challenges. When we embrace our vulnerability before God, when we cry to God and for God, we experience healing and empowerment.

2. MOVE INTO SOUL EMPOWERMENT

- Everything that has happened in your life has been for your growth, even all your trials and challenges. Reflect on what you have learned from your pain and now you can share in the world. Stand in the question" What do you God want of me today?

- Know that there is something in this world that only you can do. Even the smallest actions you do can move heaven and earth. Volunteer to be of divine service and know that God is supporting and empowering you to do what you are called to do. There will be frequent opportunities made available for you to be of service. Life often becomes easier for us to open to the glorious experience of the Divine Presence, right where we are, when we are sharing with others. We also can then better understand the purpose for the challenges we faced and what we learned from them. Because of the hardships we have endured, we have something more profound to share with others.

3. OPEN TO THE JOY OF ONENESS

- In this state of connection, we move from petitioning anything from the Creator other than the gift of closeness. It is a supreme gift to love God with no agenda other than love. This is the ultimate gift of our human existence. We came to this world to love God and know we are loved by God. In this consciousness, we know that we are taken care of, we have no need to ask God for anything. As the experience of closeness with God deepens, we experience that we are a part of God. We may even experience our true essence as love itself.

- Exert whatever you need to discipline, focus and guide your thoughts and feelings to serve the deeper desire of your soul to love God. Do not love God for any reason other than the joy of loving and basking in divine love itself.

- Take time to simply receive God's love. Place your hands on your body in a self-hug and imagine you are being embraced by the Divine. You are the beloved, and God is your Beloved. God created this world to love all of creation, including you. God wants to bestow love upon all of us but this is possible only when we are open to receive and also choose to love God and to love what is true and real. We have to invite God into our lives. **God is waiting for our invitation**. Only then may we receive the highest and deepest blessings. Take a few minutes now to open to receive the experience of being loved for who you are right now. You are indeed loved as you are right now. God does not stop loving us no matter what. We, however, can deprive ourselves of receiving God's love.

- Open yourself more deeply to the joy of this ultimate love connection with God In the prophecy of Hosea, God is telling you "I do not want to be your master, but your husband." God wants you to know God as the beloved. God wants you to know yourself as the beloved of God. This is the greatest and highest experience. This is union.

- This is Oneness. This is the Holy of Holies.
- Open to the love and joy of being close to the Divine in this way. Hug yourself for as long as you feel comfortable to absorb and internalize this love. The primary desire of your soul, your true essence, while physically embodied, is to experience this depth of love.
- Internalize this awareness of this love and presence so as to allow this awareness and connection to God to be supreme and dominant in your life, even when you are not in meditation.

WRITING MEDITATION

In addition to speaking to God in your own words, it is also good to write letters to God. Write a prayer to God. Write your own psalms to God. After doing some deep breathing to center yourself, sit in the question " What is God's message to me now? What does my soul want to say to me now?"

Lighting a candle prior may be helpful

Gaze at the candle and when you are ready, begin to write a stream of consciousness flow, imaging yourself being seen through the eyes of God and God is speaking to you. Begin this letter with these words, "This is what I want to say to you..... Continue writing until you feel complete. This writing is for you. Keep it in a journal so it is available to you in the future.

Another writing exercise is to begin writing stream of consciousness to process life events, with the following words, "Now is a time in my life when I...... continue writing until you feel complete. Keep it in a journal so it will be available for you in the future.

AFFIRMATIONS TO BE REPEATED AND MEDITATED UPON

I live my life without fear. God is with me. Because God is infinite, I let go of the fear of scarcity. Whatever I give to others is a blessing to me.

I align my personal will with Divine Will. I trust that all has happened in my life has been lovingly designed to empower me to share what I came into this world to share. God is blessing me, especially during my challenges and trials.

When I trust in God, I can let go of the burden of loss. Nothing belongs to me or anyone in this world. Everything belongs to God. God has blessed me with life. I am grateful.

The light of God flows within my body temple as my own soul. This is who I really am. I came to this physical world to embody and share God's light and love. I am this holy soul, I am this light. I am this love. Nothing that happens in this physical world can rob me of knowing this deeper truth of who I really am and who God is.

INSPIRATIONAL PERSONAL STORIES TO DEMONSTRATE THE POWER OF TRUSTING IN GOD DURING A TIME OF CHALLENGE

TRUSTING IN GOD SAVED MY LIFE

(Inspiring my professional calling)

Melinda Ribner

I could have been killed, left alone to die, totally naked in the woods, 30 minutes from where I had been abducted by knife point. I had recently turned 22 years old and the night I was abducted from a parking lot was my parent's wedding anniversary.

God knows when my body would have been found, My absence would have been noted in a few hours. My parents would have been hysterical. My brother distraught.

I knew intuitively at the time that it was best to not resist my own rape. If I fought it, I would not be strong enough to overcome him. So, I closed my eyes, I prayed, I transcended. I connected to that which was greater that what was happening in this physical world.

He raped me. I was silent. Afterwards, he proclaimed "That was good!"

As I opened my eyes, I made eye contact with him for a brief second for the first time. Because he expressed how he enjoyed raping me, I was surprised that he would then stab me in the chest and then drive off with my car, leaving me somewhere in the woods, alone, naked, and bleeding profusely.

Knowing that time was of the essence, I got myself up and quickly found a way out of the woods into a country road. As I walked down the road, I finally saw a large country house on a hill. I prayed that I could climb up the hill and make it to the house.

Grateful that I had strength to reach the house, I knocked on the door, rang the bell, a woman and her young daughter answered the door. The mother quickly ordered her daughter to go upstairs and then graciously invited me into her house. Bleeding profusely over her rug and then her couch, she called an ambulance. I thanked her for her kindness and apologized for the mess and how I ruined her furniture and rug. She kindly told me not to be concerned about that. The ambulance arrived very quickly and brought me to the Albany hospital emergency room.

As they brought me into the ER, I was surprised that they did not cover me, even though I was still totally naked. I cared and I did not care. I was absorbed in prayer. There was no one around me. I waited only a few minutes until I was seen by a few doctors.

My doctors were an Indian man and an Arab Moslem man, both foreign born with strong accents. There was not a nurse in with me. I thought the hospital might have been a little more sensitive about leaving me in a room with two foreign born men.

The Indian performed a vaginal exam and the Arab inserted a tube down my throat, as my lung had collapsed due to the stabbing. They both told me that it was miraculous that I was alive. The stabbing had just missed my heart.

After the procedure, the Arab muttered "I did not know a Jewish girl could be so brave". I marveled at the irony of this back handed compliment. I do not recall saying anything in response. I continued to pray intensely, to be connected to that what was greater than myself, greater than what was happening in my life. I was calm, actually filled with light and peace.

I was later brought into a shared hospital room with a woman who had a medical emergency during the night. Her pain, her fear and the concern of the nurses now that felt like a trauma to me. I had let down my shield of intense prayer as I tried to sleep. I was quite alarmed and triggered by the commotion taking place so close to me. The doctors and nurses hurried into the room to move her out of our shared room as quickly as possible.

Now alone, my brother was allowed to enter the room. It was the middle of the night, he had recently turned just 17 years old but he waited all night alone, directly outside my room, just to be able to see me. What a sweet wonderful brother I have. Now with him in the room, I felt safe, I felt happy, I had survived. I had endured. I would live! I was so very grateful to be alive.

What helped me to go through this rape and stabbing experience as peacefully as I did was most likely because I gratefully already established a strong and active relationship with God. When I first entered college I was confronted with so many lifestyle choices and ideologies that were new and different for me. I struggled terribly to discern what was true and real from what was false, popular and only looked good. I questioned deeply who I really was and who and what God was. My existential pain was very great. I sought guidance from the Hillel campus rabbi to address the questions about the nature of reality that so plagued me.

Unfortunately, the rabbi told me to take up swimming and not think so much, but he also advised me to read Rabbi Abraham Heschel's book *Between Man and God*. This book was a life saver for me. Heschel addressed my existential questions and inspired me to deepen my relationship with the Creator. I began to pray, meditate and talk to God in my own words almost daily for an hour each day. I even wrote poetry to God that I published in previous books I have written.

Because of these spiritual practices I discovered on my own, not only did I believe in God, I trusted in God. At the time during the rape and stabbing, I knew that I would be alright, even if my physical body would not be. Through my prayer and meditation, I already experienced myself as more than my physical body. I have to remember this important insight recently when I have had to endure substantial physical pain for longer periods of time later in my life as an older person.

When this rape happened, I had just graduated from college and was planning to go to Israel in a few months after working and earning a little money. But now it did not feel safe enough for me to travel. Instead I found employment as a case worker for the Albany County of Child Welfare for a year. This was also challenging and possibly more unsafe than Israel might have been, but it was my hometown and familiar to me. Working as a caseworker in Child Welfare was an amazing first job after college. Even though I had to visit neighborhoods that I had never visited before, neighborhoods that were viewed as unsafe in downtown Albany, and I had to interact with women who were confronting traumatic life experiences as mothers, I felt safe. I loved this job so much I decided to become a social worker.

After this traumatic experience, I knew that I wanted to help people fortify their relationship and experience with God. This was one of the many reasons I became a social worker. I wanted to share God's love and help others to deepen their connection with God, regardless of what their birth faith was.

At the very last moment possible, I applied for graduate school to become a social worker in the university close to where I lived. Just before I submitted my application and was being interviewed, the person who they had selected for this honor decided to not accept this scholarship. Surprisingly, I was given a full scholarship and a stipend because I had previously worked in Child Welfare. That was quite a gift for me. I was blessed to attend graduate school for free, on a full scholarship and spending money. I had to deal with some residual phobic fear from time to time particularly when I entered parking lots with resemblance to one where I had been abducted. Though it was challenging, taking slow deep breaths and prayer helped me to do what was necessary to get to my car.

In my last year of graduate school, a guru came to my campus. I finally heard the words my soul had hungered to hear from a human being since my first year in college when I had actively begun my search for God. I also finally met people who were also interested in their spiritual growth, loving and serving God. I even met a man I felt might be my soul mate, who grew up as a Torah religious Jew from Brooklyn who had rejected it to follow an Eastern path. I had never met a person who was brought up religious from birth. I had wanted to be religiously observant for a long time but never met anyone who was observant. My attempts to visit synagogues and be spiritually nourished there had been very disappointing.

With the companionship of this man, I now began to travel to frequent programs offered in two different ashrams while also working as a licensed social worker for almost a year after graduate school. At a certain point, my boyfriend left his position as a professor in a nearby college and went to India to live in the ashram there. I continued to attend weekend programs on my own. When I had the most powerful intense spiritual awakening experience beyond what I had ever experienced previously during a meditation workshop in one of the ashrams, one that actually awakened me to the holiness of Judaism, I decided to move to enter this ashram in West Side of Manhattan. There, I could meditate and pray daily for hours and also continue to work as a social worker outside of the ashram.

Ironically, living in the ashram actually deepened my connection to God and opened me to the power and awesomeness of Judaism. Living in the ashram also allowed me to be close to

Rabbi Shlomo Carlebach of blessed memory and attend his synagogue as the ashram was a few blocks from it. I had seen Reb Shlomo briefly before. I knew that he would be a doorway into Judaism that I was unable to find elsewhere.

After a year or so of living in the ashram, I attended a special day long program in meditation in the ashram. The whole experience of the rape and stabbing unexpectedly came up for me as if it was happening again. But now, I felt safe enough to actually feel the pain and fear that I was unable to experience previously. I even had to leave the meditation hall and go to Riverside Park. I cried deeply. I hugged trees. I cried for what I had endured. I released the pain that was not safe enough for me to feel previously. Prior to this experience, I had not cried for two years. I was just too grateful to have survived. I felt God saved my life and I did not want to feel like a victim. I wrote to the guru of the ashram in which I was living in about my experience. I wish I could remember his exact words, but it was something that what happened to my body did not and could not touch my soul. Those words comforted me and I knew it as my truth, even before he said it to me.

During the time living in an ashram, my connection to Judaism deepened as it was revealed to me in meditation to be a holy path of divine service, not just for myself, but for the whole world. Living on the west side of Manhattan I finally met Jews who loved and embraced Judaism. I moved out of the ashram immediately after attending the funeral of my beloved grandfather because I wanted to live a Jewish religious life style. I did not want to become a swami as many of my ashram friends were doing. I wanted to be a Jew.

Even though I loved living in the ashram with a disciplined daily practice, daily inspirational talks, and a loving community of seekers like myself, I felt called to living life as a Jew so as to not break the lineage of my grandfather who was a religious Jew. Under the guidance of Rabbi Shlomo Carlebach of blessed memory, I could begin to be the kind of Jew I had yearned to be, even before moving into the ashram. On my first Shabbat out of the ashram, I became religiously Torah observant.

Because I knew the firsthand the power of meditation, after a few years, I began to teach what I called Jewish meditation in 1978 and have taught almost continuously to this very day. I knew the power of meditation and wanted to share it in a Jewish way. I first began to teach Jewish meditation at the Carlebach synagogue before morning Shabbat services and once a week in the evening. After doing that, I then taught meditation at various synagogues of all affiliation. I also taught at a Jewish renewal center for summers and at new age centers. Over the years I grew in knowledge and experience about Jewish meditation and Kabbalistic teachings and wrote several books.

Eventually, I brought all the students together from all the synagogues and began to offer meditation a few nights a week in my home. At the request of the students, I offered beautiful awesome alternative gatherings for holidays that attracted Jews of all affiliation from orthodox to reform and Jewish renewal affiliation. For many years, I traveled all over the States and Israel to share Jewish meditation. I continued guiding Jewish meditation reading in Manhattan until 2006 and then in Florida and Israel when I resided there. Over the years, I have guided thousands of people, men and women.

In the early 1980's, I was hired to work several days a week as a social worker at a psychiatric clinic and teach meditation to people of all faiths because the director was familiar with my work in meditation and had witnessed my classes. At the same time, I also began a private practice as a social worker and spiritual guide, and taught Jewish meditation a few nights week in synagogues and in my home. I continue to offer counseling to individuals and couples in private practice in person, telephone or zoom. I began guiding weekly meditation on Zoom beginning at the time of Covid and continue to do so to this very day.

To me, my God connection is the most important experience I have had in my life as a human being. I knew that it was only God who kept me calm and enabled me to not freak out when I was going through this frightening ordeal. I believe that God saved my life for an important reason.

To this very day, I am devoted to strengthening my life with faith and trust, accessing my own soul, and sharing what I can with others through books, free meditation and Torah classes, and counseling.

By the way, I am sharing this story in writing for the very first time. I have only shared this story to very few people previously, but never in such detail. I do so now, because I know that many women have been raped. I want to remind them that rape does not define who they are as human beings or as women.

Melinda Ribner, Jewish meditation teacher, spiritual psychotherapist and author. www.Melindaribner.com

CHOOSING TO GO ON WITH LIFE IN JOY

Emuna Witt Halevi

I was married twenty eight years. Twenty two years of that marriage I was pregnant and nursing almost non stop. I had a great life; I had a great marriage, loved my fantastic kids, had a million guests, and our home was the headquarters for the Reb Shlomo Carlebach Chevra. My husband was my best friend, my rabbi and a good father.

Then suddenly, my husband was in trouble and life was falling apart. Events happened that went beyond all logic and the husband left the country. I could have fallen apart but there were fourteen children involved; five were married.

I didn't fall apart. We had two Rebbes in our life; one was not so available. Night after night, I went to see Reb Usher Freund, praying I could get in to speak with him. Miraculously, one night I was let in and sat down on a chair in a hallway and they said the Rebbe was asleep. It was as if I was invisible. Maybe two or three in the morning, someone asked me what I was doing there. I said I couldn't leave until I spoke with the Rebbe. Unexpectedly I heard a wedding song and I was ushered in to speak with Reb Usher. He was singing and listened to my story but somehow I didn't ask what I was supposed to do in my situation and I am not sure even what he told me. I flew home and knew that it was surreal but I didn't need to worry. And he left the world before I went again.

I was studying in a two year very difficult Keren Ariel course at Nishmat. It was a *smicha* program (really for Rabbis) in *Taharat HaMishpacha* (Family Purity). Rabbi and Rebbetzen Henkin are pioneers in educating the most brilliant women of our generation, creating the role of women *Yoetsot* (advisors) who really graduate with the knowledge to *poskin* (to decide questions of law which many women are too embarrassed to ask Rabbis). They did this quietly without a big fanfare of women's rights; they have changed Jewish history. I never told anyone that my husband left, not even my *chavrusa* (my learning partner). Being totally absorbed in learning Torah saved my life.

I travelled a few times to see the estranged husband, carrying my *Gemorah* and the *Shulchan Aruch* (book of laws), learning on planes and in airports. I felt protected and carried on with my life. I called my eldest daughter every day so I wouldn't have a nervous breakdown and also spoke with my second eldest son every day. We planned all sorts of ways to get *Aba* (his father) back. (We didn't realize he didn't want to come back.) After a year, my daughter joined the *Keren Ariel* program so I didn't have to call her; we saw each other every day and Hashem (God) gave me great strength to keep going!

Once, when I turned on a cassette tape of Reb Shlomo, what he said in his words of Torah and stories, answered all my dilemmas. What I heard was that sometimes we can spend our whole life seeing things "painted," covered up. We could be deceived without realizing it.

The second Rebbe in my life: I had the most soul shaking experience talking to a very holy, soft spoken, a real *emesdika* (truthful) Chassidishe Rebbe who actually yelled when we spoke on the phone. He changed my life and woke me up to see a different reality. At that moment I believed the Rebbe and not the husband and knew my life would never be the same. To be married, you need to believe your husband but from that moment on, I lost my unconditional trust.

We got divorced. In a million years I never imagined I would ever get divorced. I thought we'd grow old together and enjoy all the children until the end of our days. But that wasn't Hashem's plan.

What kept me on track was a psychic lady who was so wise. (A friend of a friend) I asked her why did all this happen, fourteen kids and my life falls apart? She said with great confidence that our (the ex and me) our *tikun* (fixing) was completed and I needed to go on with my life! So simple!!!

Sometimes the most simple explanation can save your life. Why go back, "could have, should have, would have…." I didn't get stuck. For a lot of people the past is like quick sand, they get so stuck, oy va voy!! I said it was a great 28 years together, but I am going on with my life.

The first Rosh Hoshana after the divorce, (around nine months later) I listened to the *Birkat Kohanim* (blessing of the Priests) and let go of any and all negativity I might have been carrying from the divorce. A new year, a new life, a new beginning, I have eight *Kohanim* sons and six daughters, *banot Kohen,* (daughters of a Kohen). What more could I ask for? I forgave the husband and didn't think about him anymore. I actually missed his davening of *Kedusha* (the special prayer in the repetition of the silent prayers. (We had a shul with a congregation of 50 (maybe more!) Reb Shlomo Chevra on Yom Tov. Why waste my time being *brogez* (angry), blaming, etc. It wasn't healthy for me or my children and I had so much to be thankful for! I let it go. As simple as that. It was good; there was chaos and now we were going to be a functional family!

Hashem found me a great job at night on the telephones; I was the best. I always got the bonus every month for bringing in the most donations! But then I fell asleep (I wasn't drinking coffee yet.) I got fired but the next day a friend who was very sick decided I needed to be her *metapelet* (caregiver) and that started twenty years of taking care of sick and older people.

On the emotional level because I had been a wife for so long, I personally needed a partner to be able to give to. Not all women need a partner/husband but it was what my soul wanted. My friends made a *shidduch* (set up a date) for me with Reuven who I knew but never thought about; obviously I was a married woman. It was someone who never had been married. Whoever thought I was crazy (how can I be with someone who doesn't know anything about marriage and I had fourteen children) I answered them laughing, "Wow, he's been waiting for me all his life!!"

Hashem was so good to me, my husband cherished me and gave me all the *kavod* (honor) in the world. The unmarried kids were jealous; we had to wait until at least one of the kids really liked him. That did happen and another two boys who were getting married told me that it wasn't respectable for me not to be married. Little by little, everyone got used to the idea and when he turned 70 and I was 54, we made a big wedding and ten out of the 14 even came to the chupah. Jokingly, under the chupah, Aaron Razel said that when you get married all the neshamot (souls) of your children come down from Heaven, but we had 10 children right there with us!!!

And the best part of the whole week was our *melave malkas* (Saturday night when you have one more meal, escorting the Sabbath Queen out.) Reuven taught me the joy of coffee and now I percolate a big coffee pot full every morning.

We had twelve fun years, simchas, children getting married, grandchildren getting married, lots of babies raining down from Heaven. Life always has challenges, maybe four years ago, my husband suddenly couldn't read and dementia set in. But I told myself, if one takes everything "*b'kalut*" (easily) and "*b'simcha*" (with joy), one can keep going with strength.

I thank God for whatever He gives me. I just want to keep my "deal" with God. If I can be a loving, patient, caring wife, I ask Hashem to please take care of all my children. There are a lot of them!! God is doing pretty well, and I am doing my best. The doctors told me my husband has to keep walking. We would go to the kotel every day, then every other day and now we try for the overview near Aish HaTorah, half way down. We still go to the Kotel twice on shabbos and it gives us *koach* (strength) for the coming week.

I transcribe Reb Shlomo's Torahs and when I edit, I read it out loud for Reuven. He still loves to learn and when I learn with *chavrusas* (learning partners) or give a zoom *shiur* (class), he joins in listening. If we do every *mitsva* (good deed) with joy, it gives us life to keep going.

I have come to realize that we really have choice on how we live our lives. We can complain about everything, find fault with everyone or we can see everything positively. We need to judge everyone meritoriously. Reb Shlomo's Torahs and Rebbe Nachman's and the Slonimer Rebbe's Torahs guide my life. Dancing and clapping sweeten the judgements and annul the bad decrees. I tell my sons to be good to their wives and my daughters are very good wives. Everyone has their "*peckalach*" (their own individual package of challenges). The "package" is exactly what we need to grow, to fix our lives, tikunim from past lives. (Actually, *tikunim* from this lifetime is enough for me.) There are some mitsvos that Hashem gives us and we feel, "Ah this mitzvah, particularly is guarding me, my children, my husband...."

But, we don't always have the same mitsvas, each year, we get different mitsvas to do. Sometimes I tell God, please, this is NOT one for me!!

I bless you and me that each day should be filled with mitsvas that we can do with joy. And that we always choose to see the good. For the first time, I wrote my story in the 31st Kol Chevra Yahrzeit Journal for Rebbe Shlomo Carlebach, that includes all Reb Shlomo Torahs that guided my life. This book can be purchased on Amazon. I love meeting new people, making new friends and would love to be in touch, emunawitt15@gmail.com.

Emuna Witt Halevi, Torah teacher and author of Kol Chevra.

MY STORY OF UNTETHERING AND RETURNING HOME

Sarah Gyampoh

There are moments in life when the walls begin to close in, when the life you've built no longer feels like a home but a weight pressing down on your chest. For me, that moment came in Ghana.

When I first moved there, I carried with me the hope that this shift – this uprooting across the ocean – would be the beginning of something new, something healing for my marriage and my family. I had five children in tow, a heart full of dreams, and the prayer that we were moving toward something better. But the truth is, my marriage was already unraveling long before our plane landed. And once we were there, in that new land, the cracks widened. What had once been whispers of doubt became an echo chamber of pain.

I remember the heaviness of those days – the loneliness, the silence that grew between my husband and me, the way hope slipped like sand through my fingers. I wanted so badly for it to work, for the story to turn itself around. But instead, I found myself at the edge of myself; tired, desperate, and asking, "Is this really all there is?"

And that was when I began to pray in a way I never had before.

I called on God with everything in me. I said, "If I am brave enough to leave this, it has to be better than this. Show me how good it can get. And let me be open to receive it." Those words were my lifeline, my anchor. And I meant them.

Each morning, before the children woke, I would unroll my yoga mat. My body was weary, but movement became my medicine. Breath by breath, I found myself again. Through meditation, I sank into silence and, in that silence, I could feel the presence of the Creator wrapping me up, whispering, "You are not alone."

Prayer and meditation became the bridge between despair and hope, between the woman I was and the woman I was becoming.

In Ghana, even as my marriage deteriorated, I found a different kind of intimacy – with Spirit, with myself. Slowly, I began to untether. Untethering is a holy process – it is the peeling away of everything you thought you had to hold on to in order to survive. It is the brave, trembling act of saying, "I choose freedom." And once I began that process, miracles started to flow.

Leaving was not easy. Imagine moving back across the ocean with five children, carrying the weight of uncertainty but also the whisper of faith. Every step felt like both a leap and a surrender. But I knew deep in my bones that I was being led.

When we returned to the United States, I was met not only with the support of friends who helped me take those first steps home but also with the steady, unwavering love of my dad. He reminded me that I wasn't starting over alone, that family and love were the soil I could root myself in again.

And then came the unfolding of miracles. My career began to grow in ways I hadn't expected. Doors opened. Connections blossomed. It was as if, the moment I chose to untether myself from what was breaking me, life itself began to rise up and meet me. Prayer had cracked me open, and the blessings had space to pour in.

Looking back now, I see how every piece of that journey was necessary. The heartbreak. The ocean between who I was and who I am now. The surrender. The bravery it took to say, "There must be more, and I am willing to step into it."

Today, I am still on that path of receiving. I begin each morning with gratitude, whispering again: Show me how good it can get. Let me be open to receive it. And life continues to surprise me; with love, with growth, with beauty I could not have scripted on my own.

My story is not just one of leaving. It is one of coming home. Home to myself, home to my children, home to a life rooted in trust and guided by Spirit. It is proof that when we dare to untether ourselves from what no longer serves us, we create the space for miracles to arrive.

And they do.

Because the truth is, triumph doesn't always look like winning the battle we thought we had to fight. Sometimes it looks like walking away, stepping into the unknown, and finding that what awaits us is better than we could have ever imagined.

I am living proof of that.

Sarah Gyampoh LMSW, RYT, RPYT, CBE Holistic Therapist.
Birth Keeper. Author

THE CALLING OF CANCER

Sara Cherem Sacal

The calling that came to me was through cancer. What began as a painful diagnosis became an unexpected invitation: to live more deeply, to heal, and to remember who I truly am.

A month before my diagnosis, I was in New York at my friend Alana's son's wedding. She looked at me closely and said: "You are too skinny. You lost iron. I think you have cancer."

Her words hurt me. I was angry at her bluntness, but I promised I would check myself.

Weeks later, during a massage, Leticia, the massage therapist, pressed her hand on my abdomen and said gently: "You have a lump in your stomach."

Days later, the truth arrived: "You have stage 4 ovarian cancer." That was the moment when the path opened. The Shabbat of Acceptance

One Shabbat changed everything. Until then, I resisted the word cancer. But that night, surrounded by prayer and silence, I whispered:

"Yes. This is my path. This is happening to me. And I will walk it with God."

It was not resignation, it was surrender. Not to illness, but to faith, to life, to the mystery of the soul.

I remember lighting the candles and feeling that the fire was also within me. In that moment, I understood that cancer was not an enemy but a messenger. That my body was asking for attention, for healing, for love.

That Shabbat, my fear softened. I was no longer running away from the word or from the truth. I chose to embrace it, to honor it, to let it teach me. And in that acceptance, I found peace.

It was a sacred turning point: the illness was still there, but I was no longer the same. I was free.

Cancer turned my hospital rooms into sanctuaries and my treatments into spaces of prayer. I also found sanctuaries in art: sitting before a Rothko and feeling its silent depth, walking through a Murakami exhibit full of color and light, or standing inside a bubble installation where infinity opened around me. Beauty, too, became medicine.

The darkest moment was not only the fear of death, but the grief of letting go; my hair falling in handfuls, my body weak, and the weight of family conflicts surfacing. Yet I chose not to collapse into victimhood. Instead, I let the illness be my teacher.

I learned that medicine and spirituality are two wings of the same bird: science cleansed my body, while faith sustained my soul.

I was held by grace in countless ways. My sister carried me through with fierce love. My mother, even with her fragility and her fall, gave me the strength of her presence. My friends across time zones prayed for me, weaving a net of light.

My friend Leticia once told me: "Life gave you very sour lemons, but you turned them into frozen lemonade in a cup of gold." Her words became a mirror of what I was learning – to transform bitterness into light, pain into offering, and illness into a vessel of meaning.

And there were unexpected angels. A homeless man not only walked me home; he stopped, looked at me with clear eyes, and said: "You will live. You will not die."

Those words stayed in my heart like a prophecy of survival. I was blessed also by children who looked at my bald head with honesty and love, and by dreams of rivers, magnolias, and renewal.

In meditation, I discovered **the void;** not emptiness, but freedom, perhaps illumination. In that vast silence, I was no longer afraid.

And nature was by my side: the forest where I walked, the deer that appeared like silent messengers of grace, and **Lulu,** the little dog who adopted me and never left my side.

Through this journey, I became more compassionate and more aligned with my purpose: to serve, to accompany others, and to create spaces of healing. My book *Reconocer* was born as testimony and as a gift, so that others facing illness may never feel alone.

I learned to accept life as it is – fragile, temporary, and full of meaning. I still grieve the visible and invisible losses, but I also celebrate love, friendship, family, and chosen community.

Today, my soul mission is clear: to live in alignment with God, to transform pain into wisdom, and to remind others that healing is possible – not only of the body, but of the heart and spirit.

Cancer was not the end of my story. It was the beginning of a deeper one.

Sara Cherem Sacal: Medical Family Therapist, writer, and author of *Reconocer* (*From Cancer to My Being*). Offering testimony and guidance for those walking through illness, grief and transformation

CONCLUSION

This book has been written from my heart to the heart of the reader. Everyone who reads this book, studies the teachings, practices the meditations and opens their hearts to learn from the personal essays will access the wisdom of their own soul and deepen their connection to God.

It is not enough to believe in God, we have to actively deepen our trust and experience of God daily. We have to get out of our way to access the holy soul within us. Our soul is not limited to the physical body; rather our soul surrounds our "body temple" as well. The soul is in the body and the body is within the soul. When we access the expanded consciousness of our own soul, we can move from a place of challenge to one of peace, protection and blessing.

Your soul is your GPS – your God Protection System- so listen to her guidance. What we need to know is already within us. We are each created with a soul purpose so we can offer something new and wonderful to the world. It does not matter what challenges we have faced or are currently facing. It does not matter what challenges the world is facing. Those who have experienced greater challenges than other people often have something even more extraordinary to offer the world.

Whatever we do in our life, let us chose that it be an embodiment of who we are on a soul level. We have to make it a spiritual practice to direct our attention to the holiness and wisdom of our own soul and to our intrinsic God connection on a daily basis, wherever we are. The challenges in the external world or within our personal lives need not determine our state of mind nor our fate.

Life is too precious to waste our time focusing on what is wrong – with ourselves, with others or with the world. Trying to understand life with our minds keeps us stuck in our heads. Wherever we are, we must open our hearts to live in the present moment as fully as possible. God is alive in the present moment. We have been given the gift of physical embodiment, not to escape or distract ourselves, but to live purposefully.

Let us always be grateful for the privilege of being human and joyful for the gifts and opportunities available to us each day as human beings. Life unfolds according to Divine Will, whether we like it or not. But we can take comfort: there is a Divine plan for the highest good – for each of us and for the world.

Our immersion in our God connection dissolves the limitations of the ego self. The stories of our pain do not define who we are on a soul level. Let not the wounding of the past distract us from the opportunity to experience the Divine Presence available in each moment. God believes in us, loves us more than our ego identity could ever do. When we get out of our own way, God will do Godly things through us.

We do not have to be perfect for God to use us for a greater purpose nor for us to fulfill our soul purpose for being alive at this time. We are essentially and sufficiently good enough to live our lives with integrity and faith. Our intrinsic value and purpose are gifts from the Creator. Anything suggesting otherwise is simply not true.

Every day we face a battle between the ego – which wants to exert power and control – and our own soul. The ego has the fantasy that it can protect us better than God. It foolishly believes that anger, anxiety, sadness and fear are forms of protection. The soul, however, knows that peace and protection comes not from battling the ego but through accepting life as it unfolds.

The soul patiently awaits the moment when we become disillusioned by the ego's attempts to make us feel worthy or safe. When we are finally willing to let go and surrender to that which is greater than the ego, we open to receive and embody the peace, wisdom and light that we seek. This is our birthright, if we choose it. Let it be a spiritual practice to always seek to heighten our consciousness of the Divine Hand in both the joyful and challenging life experiences we face in life.

Divine blessings are flowing though each of us at all times. It is up to us to get out of our own way so we may better receive what God wants to give. Receptivity to God is more powerful and sustainable than any vigorous self-effort we imagine we need to make to feel" good enough" in our own eyes.

Everything in this physical world is temporary. Thoughts, emotions and physical sensations come and go. We cannot hold onto anything forever. Yet, our Divine connection is eternal, bringing healing, joy, boundless love, inner peace and blessings to us that are not limited to the physical world.

Rabbi Moshe Luzatto in his holy book "Path of the Just" begins by reminding us that the human being was created for the sole purpose of rejoicing in God and deriving pleasure in the Divine Presence – for this is true joy and the greatest pleasure to be experienced. In spite of the tremendous personal hardships he experienced, the Ramchal, as he is called, wrote the most inspirational books, revealing both theory and practice, on how to live a holy life in the midst of challenges. He modeled this potential to us in his personal life as well.

The most supreme gift of our soul access is the taste of immortality. Because God is eternal, with no beginning and no end, when we are attached to God, when we experience God as the only true reality, we taste immortality as well, for we are a part of God. Have trust and faith that there is life after this physical embodiment.

Listen daily to the yearning of the soul. Honor her refusal to accept the divisiveness and separation in the world as truth. Through our varied life experiences, listen to the soul's remembrance of who she was before she entered the physical body. Listen to her guidance on how to walk on the path of Divine Oneness for yourself and for the world. We reach our fulfillment in the moments when our bodies, hearts, and minds align with the soul and her unity with God. This is a taste of Divine Oneness.

Our soul is God's candle in this world. When we access our soul, we radiate light. Our soul illumination helps others to access their own soul. When enough of us are awakened to the soul's truth of Divine Oneness, peace will emerge in the world.

CONCLUDING MEDITATION

To truly come close to God, to our own soul, is to taste Divine Oneness. Only then may we glimpse who really we are on a soul level. When we taste Divine Oneness as the truth while physically embodied, we feel alive and fulfilled, no matter what has happened or is happening in our life.

We experience this consciousness of Divine Oneness through meditation, prayer and doing good deeds. Jews traditionally recite the *Shema* prayer three of four times daily to access a taste of Divine Oneness. The *Shema* is a ticket to the highest spiritual consciousness we can experience as human beings.

Not only does the *Shema* tell us that there is one God, with proper intention, it reveals to us that ultimately there is only God. Only God has true reality. Human beings are essentially a part of God and not individuals with a independent existence from God. To the extent that we experience ourselves as a part of God, we become real. We taste eternity. We see and experience God in all of life.

Practice the following meditation several times each day – ideally first thing in the morning and last thing at night before sleep. And during the day if you become distracted, overwhelmed or simply want to be more focused or present, pause for a few moments and reconnect with the six words of the *Shema*.

This meditation begins by focusing on the breath. Take five deep slow breaths from the lower abdomen to the rib cage and up to the chest. Hold gently to your comfort level and then exhale. Let go of the thoughts of the day, the past, and the future. Focus on being present as fully as possible. Enjoy the gift of being present.

For this meditation we begin by focusing on the letters of the *Shema*. The *shin* and the *mem* and we substitute an *aleph* for the *ayin*, because the *shin*, *mem* and *aleph* are the mother letters of the Hebrew alphabet. If you do not know the letters, meditate on the color and sound of the letters.

ש

Visualize the shin. The shin represents the element of fire . First, visualize shin in orange light filling the head with orange light and make the sound of the shin, that is " sh". so as to purify the mind of thoughts you wish to release. Negative thoughts dissolve in the holy fire.

Repeat the second time, visualizing the entire torso filled with holy fire. Access your willingness to enter into holy fire to release what no longer serves your highest good. Release anxiety and doubt which keep you limited and fearful. Take a few deep breaths and make the sound of the Sh as you visualize yourself filled with holy fire. Repeat this two more times.

מ

Now visualize the *mem* in blue light in the solar plexus, representing the element of water, and make the sound of the mem. Mmm. Now imagine yourself by a natural body of water. Take a few moments to let go of the roles you play in your life, the clothes you wear and now see yourself totally naked before a body of water or a mikveh.

As you enter the water, access your desire to be cleansed and purified. Dunk yourself completely. Remain underwater to absorb the experience of being immersed in water-like returning to the womb, to the consciousness before your incarnation. Repeat this three or four times, chanting the sound of the *mem*-mmm) When you are ready, walk out and return to the experience of sitting with your breath.

א

Now visualize the *aleph*, the silent letter, representing the element of air above your head. Hold this visualization of the letter for as long as comfortable as you breathe deeply. The *aleph* connects us to the light before creation.

Now we are ready to chant the word of the *Shema* as we previously did with the letters. Take time to pause, listen and be receptive in the spaces between the words. When we chant the words of the *Shema*, we join the community of Jews who have been chanting the *Shema* many times daily, for thousands of years.

שְׁמַע

The first word of the *Shema* is "*Shema*" – the call to listen, to quiet the mind, to be fully present. Be with this word for a few breaths as completely as you can be.

יִשְׂרָאֵל

Yisrael – connect with the holy community of Israel who are currently chanting the *Shema* daily. Stay with the breaths to feel your belonging. The Hebrew word *Yisrael* is connected to the two Hebrew words *yashar* (straight) and *El* (God). We go straight to God, to the Creator. There are no intermediaries.

Adonai – Visualize the letters YHVH on your inner screen. And meditate on the experience of God that is beyond and greater than creation. God is transcendent. Stay with this word and the letters silently for a few moments.

אֱלֹהֵינוּ

Elohaynu, our God is intimate and personal. Take a few breaths to absorb this experience. We can always call on our God. Jews have a covenantal relationship with God. But every person can call on God. God is God for everyone.

Adonai visualizing the letters of YHVH inside the body. The *yud* in the head, the hay in the heart and vav through the torso from heart to the genitals and the hay in the waist and legs. God is immanent. God is within everyone and everything in this world. Pause for a few breaths and be with this revelation of God.

אֶחָד

Echod – One. From the divine perspective there is no inside or outside. There is only Oneness. There is only God. You can chant *Echod* a few times to meditate more deeply on the Oneness of God. God is one. God is the True reality and we are a part of this Oneness. There is ultimately only God.

Chant the *Shema* daily and slowly with or without the contemplation above.

שְׁמַע יִשְׂרָאֵל יי אֱלֹהֵינוּ יי אֶחָד

Shema... Yisrael,....Adonai.... Eloheynu,.... Adonai... Echod.

Listen Israel, The Lord Your God, the Lord is One.
Listen. God is transcendent, God is immanent. God is One.

Whisper the next line:

בָּרוּךְ שֵׁם כְּבוֹד מַלְכוּתוֹ לְעוֹלָם וָעֶד

Baruch Shem Kvod Malchuto L'olam Vaed.

Blessed is the Name of His glorious kingdom for all eternity.

We then repeat, "**You should love the Lord your God with your heart, your might and your soul**"

Soak in the vibration of love. You will naturally be filled with love of God for no reason other than you experience yourself as a part of God. God is a unity, united with all of creation and everything taking place in the world.

This love is not just commanded externally but rather this love is revelation from the experience of unity. After chanting the *Shema,* take a moment to listen - to receive guidance.

Stay in meditation for as long as comfortable. Internalize what you receive so you can embody this consciousness of love when you are not in prayer or meditation. Having tasted Divine Oneness, how do you live your life?

There will be many opportunities arising each day to express the love awakened through meditation and prayer in small and possibly large ways. Several of us will be blessed to do something meaningful of service to others.

All the good deeds we do in this world are said to carry us to a higher standing in the next world. All the suffering we experienced in this world is also said to elevate us in this journey in the next world as well.

Before a person leaves his physical body, it is customary to recite the *Shema*. Or have someone will say it on one's behalf. This is how important the *Shema* is.

Love, Miriam Shulamit aka Melinda Ribner

GLOSSARY OF TERMS

Aba (Abba): A Hebrew term for father

Achdut: A Hebrew term referring to unity, specifically the unity of the Jewish people

Adonai: A familiar name for God in Judaism, rooted in the Hebrew word for "to be"

Ain Sof (Ein Sof): The mystical term for God's infinite nature, meaning "The Limitless Light" or "Without End," representing God before any contraction for creation

Aliyah: Literally "ascent"; it refers to the act of moving to

the Land of Israel or a spiritual ascent following a descent

Am Yisrael: "The People of Israel"

Baruch Dayan HaEmet: A blessing recited upon hearing news of a death, meaning "Blessed is the True Judge"

Beit HaMikdash: The Holy Temple in Jerusalem

Bitachon: A deep level of trust in God; unlike faith (Emunah), Bitachon is the understanding that God sends challenges rather than problems

Chavrusa: A study partner for the learning of sacred texts

Chevra Kadisha: A "holy society" or group of Jewish men or women who ensure the bodies of the deceased are prepared for burial with dignity and according to Jewish law

D'var Torah: A short teaching or talk based on the weekly Torah portion or other sacred texts

Elohim: A Divine name associated with *Gevurah* (judgment, boundaries, and limitation)

Emunah: The Hebrew word for faith

Geulah: The Hebrew term for redemption

Get: A formal Jewish bill of divorce

Hashem: Literally "The Name"; a common way to refer to God without using a formal Divine name

Kaddish: A holy prayer of praise to God recited by mourners for eleven months following the death of a close relative

Kedusha: Holiness or sanctity

Kotel: The Western Wall in Jerusalem, a remnant of the retaining wall of the Second Temple and a site of intense prayer

Miklat: A bomb shelter or reinforced security room in Israel

Minyan: A quorum of ten Jewish adults required for certain religious obligations, such as the recitation of Kaddish

Mitzvah: A Divine commandment or a good deed

Neshama: The Hebrew word for the soul

Shema: A central Jewish prayer affirming the oneness of God: "Hear O Israel, the Lord our God, the Lord is One"

Shiva: The traditional seven-day mourning period following the burial of a close relative

Shloshim: The thirty-day mourning period following burial, during which some restrictions remain but the mourner begins to re-enter society

Tefillah: The Hebrew word for prayer

Tehillim: The Book of Psalms, traditionally recited for comfort and Divine intercession

Tikun (Tikkun): The concept of spiritual "fixing" or rectification of the soul or the world

Yetzer Hara: The negative or "evil" inclination within a human being

Zoche: To merit or be worthy of a particular blessing or experience

AUTHOR BIO

Melinda Ribner has taught Jewish meditation since 1978 at synagogues of affiliations, throughout America, at respected New Age centers and in many places in Israel. She received *semicha* (ordination) from Rabbi Shlomo Carlebach of blessed memory and Rabbi Zalman Schacter Shalomi of blessed memory to teach Jewish meditation and provide spiritual counsel to individuals and couples. She continues to offer free meditation sessions on zoom since the beginning of COVID. She has made available videos of short and extended sessions available at Melinda Ribner You Tube channel, also available for free.

Melinda is also a formerly licensed and certified social worker (L.C.S.W.) in private practice since 1982 and continues to use personalized meditation as part of treatment with individuals and couples. She is the author of the following books: *The Gift of a New Beginning, Everyday Kabbalah, A Practical Guide To Jewish meditation, New Age Judaism, Ancient wisdom for the Modern World, Kabbalah Month by Month, a Year of Spiritual Practice and Personal Transformation, The Secret Legacy of Biblical Women: Revealing the Divine Feminine, Biblical Women who Changed the World: Ancient Wisdom and Prophecy for today, Living in the Divine Flow, Monthly Spiritual Gifts and Blessings and now, Turning Pain into Blessing.*

To contact Melinda directly:

mindyribner@gmail.com
for speaking engagements,
meditation workshops and
counseling.

Sign up for her free newsletter at
melindaribner.com or
Melinda Ribner YouTube channel

www.ingramcontent.com/pod-product-compliance
Lightning Source LLC
Chambersburg PA
CBHW070523140726
48132CB00029B/346

* 9 7 9 8 9 9 0 6 9 6 4 9 5 *